A Buddha from Korea

A Buddha from Korea

THE ZEN TEACHINGS OF T'AEGO

Translated with commentary by

J. C. CLEARY

SHAMBHALA
BOSTON & SHAFTESBURY
1988

Shambhala Publications, Inc.

Horticultural Hall
300 Massachusetts Avenue
Boston, Massachusetts 02115

The Old School House
The Courtyard, Bell Street
Shaftesbury, Dorset SP7 8BP

© 1988 by J. C. Cleary

9 8 7 6 5 4 3 2 1

FIRST EDITION

Printed in the United States of America

Distributed in the United States by Random House
and in Canada by Random House of Canada Ltd.

Distributed in the United Kingdom by Element Books Ltd.

Library of Congress Cataloging-in-Publication Data
Pou Kuksa, 1301–1382.
  A Buddha from Korea.
    Translation of: T'aego Hwasang orok.
    1. Zen Buddhism—Doctrines—Early works to 1800.
I. Cleary, J. C. (Jonathan Christopher)   II. Title.
BQ9268.P6713 1988   294.3'927   88-17479
ISBN 0-87773-453-4 (pbk.)

CONTENTS

CONTENTS

CONTENTS

CONTENTS

CONTENTS

PREFACE

A Buddha from Korea is intended to open a window on Zen Buddhism in old Korea. The book centers on a translation of the teachings of the great fourteenth-century Korean Zen adept known as T'aego, who was the leading representative of Zen in his own time and place. This is an account of Zen Buddhism direct from an authentic source.

Few books in English dwell on any part of the Korean experience before the recent period. We might be vaguely aware that Korea has a cultural history and a continuous political tradition reaching as far back as Britain or France, but what do we know of it? What do we know of this nation we so blithely dominate and consign to the ranks of those who are "not ready" for democracy?

Through T'aego's words we can see into the mentality of his time and place, into a moment in Korea's religious and political history. The forgotten faraway land reaches us in a human voice, touching many dimensions, no longer so alien. In Buddhism, T'aego was heir to a tradition that had already crossed many national and cultural boundaries in old Asia. In T'aego's own time, the period when the Mongol empire was collapsing, international interchanges were brisk among Zen people from China, Korea, Vietnam, and Japan.

The adepts of Buddhism were the core of enlightened teachers and sincere students who were not only seekers, but finders. They knew Buddhism as a body of wisdom that was ancient in human historical terms, yet modern for being always currently engaged in a necessary course of

xi

renewal and readaptation to the times. Zen wisdom was meant to be both timely and always in essence really timeless, beyond time. The adepts did not see the Dharma (Reality, the Truth, the teaching of truth by truth) as wedded to any particular idiom or culture or social identity. They stated this in classic scriptures and proved it in deeds by propagating Buddhism in an endless variety of forms all across South and Central and Southeast and East Asia.

The real teachers expressed themselves in local terms, but were not trapped in the limitations of local worldviews. Buddhists were among the original internationalists in old Asia. The great Buddhist scriptures such as the *Lotus Sutra* and the *Flower Ornament Sutra* are testaments to the vision of the multiplicity and diversity of worlds and realities, and to the opportunities for communication among them.

As a Zen teacher, T'aego was both a man of his times, deeply involved in contemporary Korean scenes, and a Buddhist adept with timeless insight. He lived in a time of intense political upheaval, as Korea struggled to throw off foreign domination and defeat its local agents. When he saw the time was right, he did not shrink from the most dangerous of political arenas; when not active in high politics, he worked at the grassroots. Participating in the world from a Buddha's standpoint of detached compassion, he showed no fear of losing his serenity, or his life.

Can Buddhism cross yet another cultural barrier and say anything to twentieth-century people? Will we feel for T'aego's cool intensity, see the beauty of his imagery? Will his modern mentality and blunt talk surprise us? Do the metaphors of the Zen family have enough universality to get through today?

As a translator I try to deliver into our language enough of the meaning and the particular tone of the original so that the reader has a fair chance of responding to its content and intent.

To prepare the ground for new readers to follow

T'aego's words, there is an introduction to the spectrum of Buddhist beliefs and teachings, and a glossary of Buddhist names and concepts. There is information on Korean history to help make sense of T'aego's life and times, and to dispel the fantasy view of old Asia as an idyllic land of wisdom and harmony.

For readers who are familiar with the family style of Zen, T'aego's words need no introduction: as ever, "the Pure Wind is circling the earth."

All are invited: to find out something about Korea and Buddhism, to hear about T'aego himself, and to witness real Zen teaching.

ACKNOWLEDGMENTS

This project began when I could find no suitable books on Korean Zen for a course I was teaching called "Zen Buddhism in and beyond Asian History." Thus I wish to thank my students at Wesleyan University for prompting me to do more research into Korean Zen.

The scholarly books tell the same stories, mention the same personalities and famous incidents, and thus give a skeletal outline of the history of Korea and of Buddhism there, all subject to the writers' own varying interpretations and judgments. For a general orientation, I am indebted to the works of scholars like Nukariya Kaiten, Li Kibaek and Edward Wagner, and Robert E. Busswell.

But to nonspecialists, books written by and for Korea specialists are impenetrably arid, or inaccessible because of language barriers. Moreover, they often incorporate hidden suppositions about social history and mistaken concepts of Buddhism that would tend to mislead anyone who was not already familiar with Asian history and with the teachings and methods of Buddhism.

To provide materials on Zen in Korea that would be informative and usable, the logical alternative was to translate primary sources, to give direct access to the authentic spokesmen of the tradition.

The T'aego Collection (*T'aego Chip,* edited by Solso, published by Pojesa: Pyongch'ang, 1940) was one of the sources I found resting peacefully in oblivion on the shelves of the Harvard-Yenching Library. After translating excerpts from a range of Korean Zen records, I was drawn back to T'aego to translate his words in full.

I would like to thank the Library staff and particularly Mr. Kim Sungha, who helped me locate texts. Thanks also to Professor Edward Wagner, who helped me transliterate Korean names and patiently entertained my questions on fourteenth-century Korean history. Compared to these gentlemen, I know next to nothing about Korea, and my own elementary work should not be taken as a reflection of their much more learned views. Still, I must express gratitude for the help they freely gave a stranger. Errors of course are mine.

I am not a Korea specialist: I offer this book as a Zen translator. When I chance to find a remarkable jewel like T'aego's work, there is no choice but to bring it to light and share it by translating it. In Yogacara and Madhyamika studies I have been helped greatly by Nguyen Tu Cuong. In studies of Zen and Huayan Buddhism and Taoism, I owe a debt to Thomas Cleary. Naturally we all feel a tremendous obligation to the early sages and seers whose teachings we are fortunate enough to encounter: we try to meet the responsibility by making these translations and accounts of Buddhism accurate, alive, and clear.

A Buddha from Korea

T'aego's World

T'aego, a buddha from Korea, lived and worked in the fourteenth century, some eighteen hundred years after Shakyamuni Buddha had set the Wheel of the Dharma turning back in old India. Over these centuries the Buddhist teachings had spread out across Asia, developing an enormous variety of practical techniques and philosophical formulations and local cults. India and Sri Lanka, Central Asia and Iran, Southeast Asia and the islands, East Asia, Tibet, North Asia—all in time felt the influence of Buddhist images and ideas. Adapting to local outlooks in order to communicate its consistent core message, Buddhism proved able to cross the deep cultural, class, and ethnic barriers that divided old Asia.

In operation over such a vast stretch of territory and time, Buddhism naturally evolved many forms. It became institutionalized in various ways and interwoven with local feelings and styles and moods and sensibilities. This shows on the faces on the statues: in India the buddhas looked Indian, in China Chinese, in Java Javanese.

Rather than a means of transcending the world, Buddhism for most people was simply part of the scenery of their local world. It was familiar, domesticated, an emotional comforter, a set ideology, a prop for certain beliefs and attitudes and customs. Thus, as a worldly religion, Buddhism was as variegated and colorful as the world itself.

But there was a continuous inner tradition in all Buddhist lands that spoke of a basic unity underlying this great diversity of outer forms. To the adepts of the inner tradition, the diversity of true teachings was a necessary expres-

1

sion of the adaptability demanded by reality. All true teachings aim to promote enlightened awareness, but since the audience and the situation vary, so must the methods of teaching and the manner of expression. In Buddhism, this is known as the principle of *skill in means:* it is the hallmark of the true teaching (and the opposite of dogmatism).

The adepts of the core tradition took it as acknowledged fact that there would always be a tendency for worldly motivations and attitudes to surround and masquerade as true religion. They knew that even the most excellent teachings and spiritual practices could become objects of attachment and contention and blind allegiance, and thus barriers to enlightenment.

The records of Buddhism are full of detailed analyses and stern warnings on this point. But the adepts were not indignant or alarmed or dismayed by this fact. As bodhisattvas they had a cosmic time-frame and complete equanimity motivating their compassion, and they did not blame the deluded for their delusions. Sometimes they worked against certain popular beliefs and practices, but more often they worked from within to infuse local customs with whatever illumination they would bear. The true adepts were constantly mindful of the need to make a living adaptation of Buddhism to their own time and place, by whatever means were at hand. The means varied, but the intent was always the same: to enable people to open up their enlightened perception and realize their identity as buddhas.

T'aego himself was a worker in this inner tradition, and in the talks and letters and poems translated below he expresses its viewpoint with power and precision. It is not for the translator to pretend to predigest or summarize such material: it is simply too rich in meaning for that. Let the reader approach with an open heart and reap the harvest personally.

Readers who are familiar with Zen Buddhism and with

East Asian history may wish to proceed directly to the translation. For others, this introduction will fill in some basic information on three related themes: the spectrum of Buddhist teachings and beliefs, the history of Buddhism in East Asia and particular in Korea, and the life and times of T'aego himself.

THE BUDDHIST SPECTRUM

T'aego was the representative of Buddhism in a certain time and certain place: fourteenth-century Korea. As an adept of the Zen school, he participated in a centuries-old, firmly rooted, international tradition that was influential in contemporary religion and culture in China, Vietnam, and Japan, as well as Korea. The Zen masters considered themselves heirs to the original inspiration of Shakyamuni Buddha, the founder of Buddhism. To begin to appreciate the perfected synthesis of Buddhist methods which T'aego employed, we must recall some of the main currents within East Asian Buddhism.

The Coming of Buddhism to East Asia

By T'aego's time, Buddhism had been propagated in East Asia for a thousand years and more. Arriving over-land through Central Asia and by sea from South Asia, Buddhism came to East Asia at first as a religion of foreign monks and traders. Its teachings were spread in widening circles via folktales, morality plays, and images and statu-ettes illustrating the stories and picturing the great beings of Buddhism, the buddhas and bodhisattvas. Mostly un-documented, but basic to the spread of Buddhism in actual fact, were person-to-person encounters with monks and nuns and pious Buddhist layfolk. Buddhists from Central Asia and India working in translation centers in Chinese cities undertook to render the vast corpus of Buddhist scriptures and treatises into written Chinese, the language of high culture throughout old East Asia. The work of translation continued over centuries.

From the fourteenth century C.E. on, Buddhism was adopted as the state religion by many of the rulers o of the new kingdoms in North China, Korea, and Japan. Independently awakened East Asian Buddhists appeared, still venerating, but no longer dependent on their foreign mentors, and began to produce a native East Asian Buddhist literature. Buddhist temples, with their distinctive architecture and imagery, with their monks and nuns and ceremonies and chants and festivals, became a familiar sight in the major population centers. Buddhist teachings on karmic reward and punishment began to penetrate popular religion, and Buddhist rituals were gradually incorporated in the life cycle.

Long before T'aego's time, Buddhism in East Asia had come to exist as an established presence on many levels at once, both within and beyond society.

Everyday Popular Buddhism

There grew to be a broad groundwork of popular Buddhist beliefs and practices that could be found among the faithful up and down the very steep social hierarchy. Simplistic routinized religious attitudes prevailed as much among aristocrats as among commoners. The men and women who took the Dharma to heart and became adepts came from humble backgrounds as well as from the great houses.

As far as most people were concerned, Buddhism was mainly an ethical teaching, bolstered by a comprehensive set of rituals for every occasion. The most basic Buddhist code prohibits killing, stealing, lying, illicit sex, and intoxication. Believers were encouraged to show compassion to all around them, to strive for harmony, and to be willing to perform altruistic service for the community. If living as laypeople, they were supposed to carry out the social obligations appropriate to their station in life: peasants should be good peasants, hardworking and uncomplaining; merchants should be good merchants, honest and charitable; aristocrats should be good aristocrats, just and merciful, avoiding war and coercion as much as possible, employing force only in righteous causes; women should be good wives and mothers, nurturing their children and infusing their households with Buddhist piety.

For those who left home to become monks and nuns, the prescribed codes of conduct (called the *vinaya*) were very strict and detailed. Self-denial and restraint were mandatory for monks and nuns. They were expected to be good monks and nuns in order to "repay the benevolence" of their relatives and the ruler for having permitted them to abandon normal social obligations.

Buddhist ethical teachings were grounded in the idea that in the natural course of cause and effect, wrong conduct would bring punishment and good conduct would accrue merit. *Karma* means "deeds" or "actions." Actions bring inevitable results: karmic reward or punishment.

A basic notion in popular Buddhism is the transfer of merit. The karmic merit gained by charitable works or religious observances could be transferred to others (for example, to living or deceased relatives, to patrons, to future generations) to help ameliorate the consequences of their karma. Monks and nuns were supposed to transfer to their kinfolk part of the merit gained through lives of religious dedication, thus contributing to their spiritual welfare, in lieu of the material support they might not be giving. Families might not object to children becoming monks and nuns, despite the worldly loss, when they believed this worked to their own karmic benefit.

In East Asian popular Buddhism, karmic consequences are mostly seen as operating in the family line, so that the results of the sins of the ancestors would be visited upon their descendants. As with our "poetic justice," in the popular conception of the workings of karma, the punishment fits the crime. Using this eminently flexible frame of reference, people could explain to themselves many of the vagaries of family fate and fortune and the dynamics of personality patterns. People in a position to "get away with" some evil might desist, knowing that their children and grandchildren would ultimately have to suffer. People of power and means might be moved to contribute to the Buddhist community and its charities, to help offset the karmic burden they felt they had incurred for themselves and their families.

Visitors from the stars might observe that the Buddhist teaching on karma and its consequences, like other classical ethical teachings that have been spread here in our world, is at once a shrewd device to frighten people away from their destructiveness and folly, and a straightforward announcement of certain plain facts.

But the theory of karmic reward and punishment could also be twisted this way and that to suit the deluded convenience of the moment. Any outcome could be justified retrospectively. In particular, the idea of karma was used to justify the status quo of unequal ranks in society: "The poor deserve their misery, the nobles their power and luxury." On a personal level, people could complacently say, "My past karma has made me what I am now, however bad, so how can I change?" Or they might try to buy out of the results of their bad karma by paying for rituals.

Within the framework of reward and punishment for deeds, ordinary Buddhists paid for, attended, and took part in ritual performances where they aimed to accumulate merit and dissolve away past evil karma. This was the major theme in Buddhist rites for the dead, whether at funerals or commemorative ceremonies on the anniversaries of the deaths of particular people, or at large-scale annual public ceremonies to comfort all the dead departed. Ritual in general was seen as a way to gain merit, and lay Buddhists within the limits of their means regularly hired monks and nuns as ritual specialists, to preside over ceremonies and read from the holy scriptures. Aristocrats had private temples on their estates and kept monks and nuns in residence to chant scriptures, perform rites, and deliver homilies to the household and its dependents.

It appears that in many lands in many times, ordinary Buddhists often took a mechanical attitude to religious observances. Buddhist rituals that were long established eventually were experienced as over-familiar and routinized, vaguely comforting, but rather meaningless. There would be little motivation left except the inertia of tradition: the professional needs of ritual specialists, and the habitual mind-set among the believers that outward performance would somehow bring religious gain automatically.

Ritual and ceremonial forms usually started out as means to dramatize the Buddhist message and focus people's attention on it, and to assemble the community for some harmonious sharing. But even rituals designed or inspired by great teachers would become vitiated when people took part with a shallow self-seeking attitude. In this way a given ritual would gradually lose its original power and become part of the ordinary scenery of the world. This is why Buddhist history is punctuated by regular cycles of renewal and reworking of forms, and the leading teachers have talked so much about the danger of sanctifying externals and missing the original intent.

In step with the mechanical, self-seeking approach to ritual among the laity, the clergy would be poisoned by a payment-for-service mentality. Rather than acting as channels for the Buddha Dharma, monks and nuns would become absorbed in seeking reputation and patronage. They would learn to be psychological manipulators playing on people's fears and uncertainties. East Asian popular literature often mocked irreligious monks and nuns: the lecherous monk plotting a seduction, or the nuns at a rich lady's mansion arguing over how to split a fee. Adepts in every generation warned that the real enemies of Buddhism were not its overt opponents, but rather those monks and nuns who had the form but not the essence, who shaved their heads and wore religious garb, but were no different from ordinary people, who brought discredit on the Dharma by their avarice, power hunger, gluttony, and lust.

Institutionalization

People made donations to monks and nuns and temples, hoping that they could buy out of the results of bad karma. Such conscience-money funded a lot of Buddhist building activity, a lot of art and sutra copying, many charities and relief efforts. It paid for the incense and flowers and candles and robes used in innumerable rituals with which ordinary people marked key occasions. It fed and clothed most monks and nuns. Gifts coming from the people at the top, the kings and queens and nobles and warlords who disposed of wealth that was massive in the context of the times, enabled some Buddhist temples to build up large permanent endowments of landed property, money, and other assets.

Thus it came to be that major Buddhist temples in the East Asian lands normally collected substantial rents in kind, enjoyed tax exemptions, and controlled large numbers of bound laborers. Rich temples were usually well-connected politically, with powerful protectors among the elite. Besides being landlords, temples might operate mills for grinding grain or pressing oil, brew soy sauce or rice wine, or operate craft workshops. Temples often served as travelers' inns and meeting places. Before banking arose in secular society, Buddhist temples were centers of moneylending, with both the institutional continuity and the liquid assets to extend credit. In many areas Buddhist temples became the sites of periodic markets, where local people met to trade and gossip and be entertained.

For Buddhism, such worldly prosperity was a mixed blessing. By being institutionalized, Buddhism was accorded a defined place in society, sometimes a highly venerated and ostensibly influential place. Buddhist teachers thereby gained access to the various levels of society, and had recognized channels through which to propagate their message. Equipped with worldly wealth, the Buddhist establishments could provide colorful religious displays and pay for the reproduction of Buddhist texts and images. They also had the means to organize charities and to fund local public works.

But institutionalized Buddhism was always at risk of becoming imbued with secular attitudes and fatally entangled in worldly power struggles. Lordly donors might "give" property and convert mansions to temples in order to shelter and perpetuate their wealth. Self-interested cliques of big patrons and manager-monks might struggle for control of a temple's assets to manipulate for their own gain. Temple overseers might become hard-hearted masters exploiting their serfs and novice-monks.

The rulers of secular society could scarcely overlook the political implications of a wealthy Buddhist establishment within the realm, controlling substantial resources and labor power. East Asian rulers often acted to curb or control institutionalized Buddhism. At times there were purges of its clergy and confiscations of its accumulated wealth. Laws were written to limit the numbers of people who might be ordained as monks and nuns and to regulate the building of new temples. Rulers tried to ensure that the existing Buddhist establishment was loyal to the regime and served state purposes: the major temples complied by holding periodic ceremonies for the defense of the realm and for the longevity of the ruler.

By becoming linked to the secular power-holders, the Buddhist institutions were often drawn into their political conflicts. In the early phases of the introduction of Buddhism into the East Asian lands, contending factions of aristocrats struggling for supremacy often adopted pro- and anti-Buddhist stands as part of their rivalry. The ascendancy of anti-Buddhist factions could then result in attacks on Buddhist clergy and institutions. Even in periods when Buddhism held an honored place in public life, it was a common pattern for the reigns of rulers who were particularly avid patrons of Buddhism to be followed by periods in which the government renewed its efforts to hold Buddhism in check.

In China the state many times attempted to set quotas on the numbers of monks and nuns and temples, to require government permits for the clergy, and to outlaw private temple-building. In Korea and Vietnam and Japan, successive new regimes, on coming to power, tended to redirect patronage and create a new layer of Buddhist institutions beholden to themselves. Temples associated with the rule of their overthrown adversaries might be taken over and rededicated, or looted and destroyed, or simply deprived of their privileges and income and left to languish. When secular power was fragmented, and local warlords struggled for control over the land, as in medieval Japan and Korea, some major Buddhist monasteries went so far as to fortify themselves and maintain their own armed forces, in an attempt to fend off encroaching rivals and preserve their own holdings.

Buddhist adepts often spoke out on the insidious dangers of worldly prosperity for the Dharma. They warned monks and nuns not to get sidetracked into lives of idle luxury or self-aggrandizing ambition. For the laity, the leading teachers pointed out the traps of mechanically participating in rituals or giving alms in expectation of personal gain. According to the Great Vehicle teaching on charity, everything depends on the correct unselfish attitude; otherwise, bad karmic consequences ensue.

Zen master Nanquan (747–834) said, "If the one making the gift is thinking of giving, he enters hell like a shot. If the one receiving the gift is thinking of getting, he is bound to be reborn as an animal." There is a famous Zen story about Liang Wudi, emperor of South China (r. 502–549) and an extravagant patron of Buddhism. The emperor told Bodhidharma (the ancestral teacher of Zen) that he had built countless temples and had had numberless monks ordained, and asked, "What merit was there in this?" Bodhidharma said, "There was no merit."

Such sayings from the core of the tradition make it plain that from the point of view of the adepts, the real flourishing of Buddhism cannot simply be equated with its worldly prosperity or acceptance among the political elite, or even with the prevalence of Buddhist-derived forms in society at large.

Many modern attempts to trace the history of Buddhism have fallen into the fallacy of judging the rise and fall of Buddhism in a given country as a function of its acceptance and level of patronage by the social elite. For one thing, the beliefs of the social elite are much easier to trace, because they are better documented than religious history at other social levels. Moreover, modern ideas about human nature shape the historical account. The assumption is made that there could have been no other motivation among religious leaders but to win a following and attract patronage and become rich and powerful. Thus, everything must be ideological manipulation or self-deception.

To modern people, this guiding image is eminently commonsensical, and is borne out again and again in recent examples. It is a view sanctified by the eighteenth-century Western Enlightenment rationalists, and adopted intuitively by us, their latter-day descendants, who are disillusioned with rationalism, let alone religion.

This image fits many phenomena in East Asian Buddhist history. We see it in popular Buddhism, with its everyday sophistries and shallow routines, its mechanical attitude toward ritual, its service-for-hire clergy. It is easy to see in the so-called Buddhism of courtiers and kings, who tried to bolster their power on earth through supernatural means. It is tempting to imagine in the rebel Buddhism of millenarian movements, which mobilized people around beliefs in predestined impossible utopias. There is a lowest common denominator running through all these phenomena: the self-interested attempt to use religious means for worldly ends.

But when we bring into view the recorded teachings of the core teachers, our cynical modern interpretation loses its plausibility. Look again at Nanquan's saying above. Was he really trying to curry favor with the temple patrons that day, when he told them their attitude toward giving would send them straight to hell? Let anyone read even once through the profoundly unsettling teachings of T'aego or the other Zen masters. Then see if it still seems plausible that T'aego and the others were out to attract a following, either as cynical cult impresarios or as self-deluded zealots.

The Buddhist Scriptures

T'aego's teachings reflected current trends in East Asian Buddhism, and his audience took for granted certain notions of the Dharma contained in the Buddhist classics. To follow his meaning, modern people need some information about basic Buddhist ideas that were common knowledge among T'aego's listeners.

The Buddhist teaching emanated from India in a rich variety of forms and formulations. Six centuries of elaboration and development had taken place in the Indian cultural sphere before Buddhism spread into East Asia in the third and fourth centuries C.E. So East Asians were introduced to an enormous variety of Buddhist materials: from detailed codes of monastic discipline to grand depictions of universal salvation, from treatises in analytic philosophy to the tableaux of meditations in the sutras. Up through the eight and ninth centuries, even after acculturated East Asian forms of Buddhism had appeared and taken root, there were new pulses, new visions of the Dharma coming out of India to give fresh impetus to Buddhism across East Asia, and to spark further developments.

Learned Buddhists in the Far East interpreted this diversity of religious method and lore as a reflection of the

principle of skill in means: different Buddhist teachings
were seen as representing different phases of the Buddha's career and as addressed to audiences with differing
potentials. But behind them all was always a single intent:
to enable people to open up their enlightened perception.

There were many schemes for classifying the teachings
put forward, varying in detail, but here is a summary con-
sensus of the Huayan and Tiantai philosophers' view:

The teachings that stressed release from the cycle of
suffering through strict discipline and meditation at the
individual level were categorized as the elementary forms
of Buddhism, the Buddha's preliminary revelations. To
get people moving, this level of teachings held out the
prospect of salvation beyond the world, of nirvana apart
from samsara, which is the cycle of birth and death. These
teachings stressed the process of interdependent causation
underlying all mental states and all experience. To break
the cycle of ignorance and craving and suffering, they
prescribed a lengthy process of scrupulous practice: many
lifetimes, or even eons, of accumulating merit through virtuous conduct and meditation. These teachings were
sometimes called the Lesser Vehicles: not to deny their
(provisional) validity, but to point out that they should be
employed as stepping stones, and not imagined to be final
truths or ultimate destinations.

At the next level were the elementary teachings of the
Great Vehicle. These widened the focus to the objective
of salvation for the whole community. They teach that
there is one reality pervading everything, and that our true
nature is to be enlightened to it, to be aware of our oneness
with it. Buddha is glimpsed as a transhistorical reality, of
which the historical Buddha Shakyamuni and all other enlightening beings are local particular embodiments.

In this category belongs the *Vimalakirti Sutra,* a scripture
with major impact in the implanting of Buddhism in East
Asia. Vimalakirti (whose name means "Pure Name") is
shown as an enlightened layman who lives in ordinary soci-

ety but shares in the highest wisdom of the buddhas. The scene is set as his house magically encompasses a vast supernatural assembly and huge cosmic thrones: a metaphor for his integration of the worldly and the world-transcending. Another sutra in this set is the *Sutra of Queen Shrimala,* which teaches that the infinite array of appearances of the phenomenal worlds in fact comprise the womb from which the enlightened ones come forth. This womb is the matrix of reality, which contains all things and all the experiences of all beings. This level of teaching, rich in both imagery and metaphysics, was said to be both particular and general and to cover all sorts of potentials.

A further level still is the Buddhism of the so-called perfection of wisdom, or *Prajnaparamita,* literature. There is a multitude of sutras in this class, some very short, some very long, widely known and recited down through East Asian Buddhist history. These scriptures reveal the limitations of conceptual thought and establish that all apparent (mental and physical) phenomena are empty. By this they mean that all phenomena are temporary assemblies of causal factors, and lack permanent independent identities beyond that. In the Buddhist sense, true emptiness is not a blank vacuity, but is inherent in the lack of fixed identity in the flux of phenomena: this emptiness contains and pervades all things, and is their essence. This is not emptiness as opposed to form, but the emptiness inherent in all temporary forms: "Emptiness is form, form is emptiness."

This view of emptiness is basic to the Great Vehicle ideal of the bodhisattva, the enlightening being, who stays in the world to work for the salvation of others. The selflessness and detachment that come with the realization of emptiness are the basis for the bodhisattva's true compassion, which is founded not on sentimental wishes, but on an accurate appreciation of possibilities. The bodhisattvas do not seek nirvana beyond the world, but function in the world as enlightening beings, mindful all the while that they themselves, the beings they save, and the whole pro-

cess of salvation and the infinite array of worldly forms
and happenings are all essentially empty.

The ultimate level, known as the round or complete
teaching, is expounded in the the *Lotus Sutra,* the *Nirvana
Sutra,* and the *Huayan Sutra.* These scriptures give the
whole picture of the Buddha Dharma as a cosmic enterprise of enlightenment, which proceeds on all levels at
once, in countless worlds and times.

Enlightened beings of the past, present, and future are
shown witnessing and joining in the same universal illumination. A multiplicity of worlds is shown all at once: each
world with a buddha appearing in it to preach to the beings there, each the scene of all phases of the teaching of
enlightenment, each a particular environment, yet all sharing in a universal process. All the buddhas in all these
worlds intercommunicate, and share an existence beyond
time and space. The round teachings reveal the positive
qualities of buddhahood: enlightenment is eternal, pure,
blissful, and personal.

From the Huayan comes the image of Indra's net, to
express the interpenetration of all realms of existence. Picture a vast network, extending to infinity in all directions.
At every node of the net is a jewel. Every jewel reflects all
the surrounding jewels at the neighboring nodes: and in
each reflection appear the reflections of all the jewels that
surround that jewel . . . and so on, ad infinitum. Each jewel
is at once the center of its own array and a satellite in other
arrays, depending on the perspective. All time-frames, all
moments of all beings' individual life experiences, all histories of all worlds: all reflecting each other, these are dis-
played and contemplated as facets of an all-encompassing
whole. All particular actions and endeavors in the propagation of enlightenment, and all the levels of the
bodhisattva's progress and deepening realization and
growing wisdom, are seen as aspects of the concentration
of Samantabhadra, the Universally Good One.

There is no real way to summarize the Buddhist sutras:

they already *are* summaries. The scriptures must be experienced to be appreciated. One look at the sutras will confound the usual bland image of Buddhism and all attempts at philosophical paraphrase. As they say in Zen, "The lion's roar bursts the jackals' brains." Those who are not afraid to encounter the full force of the round teaching of Buddhism are invited to look at the English translation of the *Huayan Sutra* (see Thomas Cleary, trans., *The Flower Ornament Scripture,* 3 vols. [Shambhala Publications, 1984–1987]).

In East Asia, the sutras provided a fundamental basis of teachings that could be drawn on in many forms. Chanting the scriptures, or hiring monks and nuns to do so, was a near-at-hand means for the faithful to acquire merit. Many Buddhist monks and nuns specialized in reciting or lecturing on particular sutras. Through them, through marketplace storytellers and through written texts, the dramatic scenes and philosophy of the sutras were disseminated high and low: some sections of some scriptures became extremely well known, some episodes entered popular literature, and certain texts were venerated and thought to have magic powers. As predicted in the sutras themselves, their teachings were received among the populace in various ways at various depths. People might take them for everything from moral lessons and edifying fables, to charters for particular beliefs and observances, to maps of the ultimate zones of awareness. They were codes with many messages.

All levels of East Asian Buddhism built on the sutras. The religious concepts and story-lore and art of popular Buddhism took their start from the sutras. In the intermediate period of the introduction of Buddhism, there were distinct East Asian schools of specialists in the philosophy of particular scriptures and treatises. Many East Asian Buddhists made the long hazardous journey to Central Asia and India to bring back authentic texts. Temples collected copies of scriptures, and rulers sponsored vast compendium editions by paying for the printing blocks and arranging for copies to be printed and distributed to major temples. The first printed books were Buddhist sutras.

Both the enduring practical currents of East Asian Buddhism, Pure Land and Zen, were rooted in the scriptures, but in different ways.

Pure Land Buddhism

In the sutras of the Buddha of Infinite Life, Pure Land believers found a promise that even sinners could gain salvation by relying on the power of Amitabha Buddha's vow to deliver all beings. Amitabha (whose name means "Infinite Life") grants rebirth in the Western Paradise to all those who invoke him. There in the Pure Land with Amitabha, enlightenment becomes possible for people lacking the strength or discipline to become enlightened here on our earth, the world the Buddhist scriptures named "Endurance." All grades of people, even the hopeless reprobates, are guaranteed ultimate salvation through faith in Amitabha.

The typical Pure Land practice is chanting the name of Amitabha, which can be done inwardly or aloud, alone or in groups. The Pure Land founders advocated reciting the buddha-name as a method simple enough for the people of the later ages, who were not up to the rigors of classic Buddhist discipline and meditation.

Pure Land Buddhists in East Asia often formed laypeople's associations where they met regularly with other believers to chant the buddha-name, and to direct their minds toward Amitabha's Pure Land in the West. Pure Land groups might continue generation after generation, with their own leaders, ritual forms, meeting halls, and even mutual aid funds for their members.

Belonging to such a group not only helped strengthen members' religious faith: it could also provide an important social support network. Periods of increased turbulence and insecurity in secular society were often accompanied by an upsurge in Pure Land belief. Through Pure

Land societies, beleaguered peasants and townspeople could find psychological comfort: they might reconcile themselves to hopeless worldly circumstances by shifting the focus of their lives to rebirth in the Pure Land.

The quality and intensity of Pure Land faith naturally varied greatly from person to person. For some, reciting the buddha-name was a superficial mechanical act; for others, it was an act of fervent hope and devotion. No doubt the feeling achieved through group chanting helped sustain and soothe many believers. Pure Land biographies often feature deathbed scenes: after a pious lifetime of reciting the buddha-name, the dying person sees the Pure Land opening up and Amitabha coming to receive her or him. Such stories offered more proof to the faithful that rebirth in the Pure Land was to be their reward.

Among some Pure Land adepts theory and practice were extended far beyond what the simpler believers held to. Here the recitation of the buddha-name became real buddha-remembrance, bringing the practitioners out of their conditioned minds into mindfulness of reality. Rebirth in the Pure Land was seen as a moment-to-moment event, to be achieved by purifying the mind through single-minded concentration on the buddha-name. Full realization for these adepts meant return from the Pure Land to help the people in the ordinary world: at this stage, neither pure lands nor impure lands are a barrier or point of attachment.

This vision of Pure Land Buddhism facilitated the linked teaching of Zen and Pure Land methods: many East Asian Buddhist teachers from the tenth century on were at home with both Zen and Pure Land practices, and emphasized one or the other or both together as the occasion required.

Zen Buddhism

Among all the forms of East Asian Buddhism, it was the Zen school that had the most profound impact on the region's high culture and philosophy.

The pioneers of Zen drew on the classic Mahayana sutras, particularly the *Lankavatara Sutra*, the *Diamond Sutra*, the *Sutra of Complete Enlightenment*, the *Vimalakirti Sutra*, the *Surangama Sutra*, the *Nirvana Sutra*, and of course the *Lotus Sutra* and the *Huayan Sutra*. They took for granted the analysis advanced by the Madhyamika school of Indian Buddhism, which refutes all conceptualizations and shows the inability of propositional logic to encompass reality. The Zen adepts also took over the analysis of experience made in the Yogacara school. Here the presumed outer reality we think we perceive is shown to be a construct produced by the interaction of form, sense faculties, and various levels of conditioned consciousness. For their all-embracing world-view, integrating all levels and all particulars, the Zen masters had the Huayan teachings.

The diverse meditation techniques and perspectives of Zen were in fact drawn from the classic scriptures, yet the early formulators of Zen spoke of it as a separate transmission outside the scriptural teachings. What did they mean by this? Their aim was to point directly to the human mind, without setting up any verbal formulations as sacred. Zen developed, according to its adepts, not to deny the validity of the sutras, but because people were not carrying out the teachings contained in the sutras. Zen teachers wanted people actually to apply these teachings in everyday life, not merely to worship the sutras as sacrosanct texts or remote myths. To the Zen adepts, it was a sure sign of basic incomprehension to suggest that Zen and the sutras could be at odds with each other. To them, Zen was nothing but a fulfillment of the intent of the sutras. In practice Zen masters made frequent use of texts like the

Lankavatara and *Surangama* sutras, which read like compendia of meditation methods.

Zen teachers stressed that the buddhas began as human beings, that enlightenment is within reach in a single lifetime for those who are dedicated enough. "A complete human is a buddha, a complete buddha is a human being." They interpreted the scenes in the scriptures as metaphoric descriptions of states experienced along the path. They wanted people to find buddha within them, that is, to find their own inherent enlightened nature. The buddhas and the bodhisattvas in the sutras were to be emulated, not just venerated. To advanced students, Zen teachers spoke of transcending the buddhas, to stress the need to reach one's own independent realization.

Apart from a scattering of enlightened lay people (whose backgrounds are more diverse), almost all the Zen masters whose biographies are recorded began as ordinary monks or nuns. As such, they had spent years observing strict discipline while they studied Buddhist scriptures and carried out the prescribed monastic routines. While still young they generally traveled widely, seeking instruction and hoping to be accepted as students by reputable masters. Their sincerity and dedication were answered when they met with the opportunity to serve and to receive intimate-level instruction from enlightened teachers. Zen teachers did not accept all comers: those who were accepted they spurred on with a merciless compassion that did not compromise with conventional habits and feelings. "I would rather accept the torments of uninterrupted hell, than portray the Buddha Dharma as a human sentiment and thus blind people's eyes."

Most who found the Path went through long rigorous periods of intense meditational effort. Progressions varied from individual to individual, but typically they passed through many deepening stages of insight, and experienced more and more encompassing enlightenments. At every stage, they turned to experienced teachers or the

scriptures to attest to their attainments and to guide them
further. Many who thought they had already reached the
ultimate level had their pretensions shattered again and
again by relentless teachers who drove them on till they
finally did arrive. "One truth runs through ancient and
modern: contact with reality is Arrival." The techniques
of Zen teachers were compared to forge and bellows, hammer and tongs—tools by which the learner was refined and
shaped. The Dharma itself, the great treasury of the teachings bequeathed by enlightened predecessors, gave the
ruler and compass and measuring square by which inconceivable experiences could be judged objectively.

According to the principles of Zen, only those with
genuine independent awakening and a thorough mastery
of the Buddha Dharma were considered qualified to become teachers. Enlightened teachers painstakingly prepared their special successors, often over decades. Not
every person of insight was intended to become a public
teacher. Real adepts were in no hurry to set themselves
up as teachers, to become well known, to attract a following. Usually the best Zen teachers were very difficult to
approach unless the seeker was absolutely sincere. "We do
not portray the Dharma as a human sentiment and sell it
cheap."

Given the priorities of the Zen life, fame and a reputation for holiness could be burdensome, attracting un-
wanted unproductive attention. Zen masters often refused
invitations from powerful would-be patrons, or had to be
coerced into coming to court. In Zen parlance, any monk
or nun who sought patronage for the sake of living com-
fortably would be called someone following the wheel of
food, not the wheel of the Dharma. But in certain situations genuine Zen masters did utilize their reputations to
speak out publicly, to occupy positions in institutions, to try
to influence customs to guide the Buddhist community,
and to intervene in politics.

The traditional account traces the beginning of the Zen

school to the arrival of an Indian adept called Bodhidharma in sixth-century China. He met with the emperor of South China, a patron of Buddhism, but the emperor did not understand his message, so he left for North China, where he absorbed himself in meditation and awaited a worthy successor. At the beginning of the eighth century, Zen was among the schools receiving imperial patronage in China. By the ninth century, Zen as a distinctive school within Buddhism was being propagated in many centers in China, and had spread to Korea and Vietnam; in the twelfth century, it reached Japan.

A body of Zen literature grew up consisting of biographies of Zen teachers, their recorded sayings and poetry, their public talks, their letters, and the lessons they imparted to the congregations at the temples where they stayed or the centers they built. There are many themes: the limitations of conventional thinking, the transcendent intent of the buddhas, how to meditate, how to understand the sutras, how to live as monks and nuns, how to find enlightenment in lay life. In time there developed also an extensive tradition of commentary on earlier Zen sayings and teaching cases, and collections were assembled of classic sayings and stories and comments.

Zen literature became renowned throughout East Asia for its intriguing subtlety and direct, striking metaphors. This was the intellectual edge by which Zen entered into Chinese high culture, a culture long enamored of subtle words. When Chinese culture was in vogue with the upper classes in Korea, Vietnam and Japan, Zen-influenced art and literature and philosophy came along with it.

East Asian elite thinkers who opposed Buddhism easily dismissed the extravagant imagery of the sutras as worthless fantasies fit only for the ignorant lower orders. What particularly disturbed them was Zen, which held a fascination for many of the best minds among the elite. They disapproved heartily as they saw Zen language and ideas filtering into their precious high culture.

The Three Religions

There was a long history of interaction among the three great religious traditions of East Asia, Taoism, Confucianism, and Buddhism. With the rise of Zen to intellectual prominence by the tenth century, both Confucianism and Taoism were reshaped under its influence. Though Taoism employs different language and metaphors, by the twelfth century the new schools like Complete Reality Taoism shared a recognizable resemblance to Zen, as well as the same fundamental message. Within Confucianism, attitudes toward Buddhism varied widely, from intransigent animosity to open-minded respect. But even among the committed philosophical opponents of Zen, we find the dimensions of the discussion have expanded under Buddhist impact and the conceptions of Confucian self-cultivation have shifted in the direction of Zen meditation. From the tenth century on, there were many advocates of "harmonizing the three religions into one." They taught that the three faiths were compatible in basic purpose and complementary in practice: Confucianism for managing the world, Buddhism for transcending the world, and Taoism for nurturing the life-energy.

Some schools of Confucianism were open to Buddhist influences, and saw a fundamental harmony between the substance of the teachings of Buddha and the teachings of China's sage, Confucius. For example, to them the Buddhist ideal of the bodhisattva was akin to the Confucian value of *ren,* human fellow-feeling or benevolence, and Buddhist meditation was paralleled by Confucian practices of composing and calming the mind. They brought to the fore passages in the classics that they read as being equivalent to their Buddhist analogs. Confucians like this often associated with Zen teachers and combined Buddhist and Confucian methods of self-cultivation.

Other Confucian thinkers repudiated Buddhism. Those concerned with statecraft criticized Buddhism for economic parasitism, and pointed to its institutional wealth and unproductive clergy. They saw it as unseemly to have another focus of loyalty in society besides the emperor. These Confucians might have liked to rid China of Buddhism, but they could not advocate attacking something so deeply rooted among the people; this would invite chaos. At most, they proposed to limit the numbers of temples and clergy, and to let Buddhism decline by slow natural attrition. When attacks on Buddhist institutions came, they were generally brief campaigns launched by aristocratic rulers and warlords whose aim was to expropriate material wealth, or to strike at rival power-bases, certainly not to stamp out Buddhist beliefs among the people.

There were Confucians who made a philosophical case against Buddhism. According to them, popular Buddhism was mere vulgar superstition, holding out to the ignorant lower classes a promise of release from suffering. The sutras they saw as incoherent and unbelievable, foreign nonsense far beneath comparison with the Chinese classics. For these Confucians, Zen was the real moral threat to cultured people: crazy libertine Zen, nihilistic and antinomian, rejecting all human norms, all proper standards of right and wrong. These Confucians advised right-thinking gentlemen to shun Zen altogether: otherwise, they might very well be seduced by it, as so many had been.

Buddhist teachers never responded with a critique of Confucianism. They generally accepted it as a local version of the worldly truth, valuable in its own sphere for cultivating basic social morality, and compatible with the more comprehensive vision of Buddhism. Quoting selectively from the sayings of Confucius and Mencius, Buddhists appeared to take it for granted that these sages had intended to communicate virtually the same message as the Buddhist enlightened ones. It was common to find East Asian Buddhist teachers urging upper-class audiences to live up to Confucian standards of humanity and righteousness.

There were Buddhist writers who refuted the Confucian critique of Buddhism by simply pointing to the bodhisattva ideal and the Great Vehicle goal of universal salvation. But mainstream Buddhists never attacked Confucian morality itself (though they did deny its claims to ultimacy). There were many Buddhists as well as Confucians who saw the underlying harmony of the two religions and worked to keep up contacts with the other side. Many famous Zen teachers from privileged social backgrounds had received Confucian educations, and knew the Confucian classics by heart. For them to use Confucian concepts with certain audiences was part of their expedient means, "putting on an old granny's shawl to go visit an old granny."

Rebel Buddhism

Although the Buddhist establishment usually cooperated with the state, there were other forms of popular Buddhism that presented a political threat to the authorities. Among the common people there were many variants of millenarian Buddhism. These sects taught their followers to expect the (more or less imminent) coming of the future buddha Maitreya, who would establish a new era of justice and plenty here on earth. By implication, the present rulers were corrupt tyrants, doomed to fall, and the present political order was part of the present evil era that was destined to be superseded. The millenarians had their own cosmic timetable for the overthrow of the status quo.

The ruling groups were keenly aware of the political danger of such doctrines and attempted to stamp them out. The government decreed legal penalties: death for the teachers and exile for the followers, destruction of all heretical scriptures and images and meeting halls. Spokesmen for the Buddhist establishment condemned them as heretical. Because millenarian groups were persecuted by the authorities whenever they came to light, they existed clandestinely under a shifting variety of names. In the Chinese law codes, they were grouped under the term *zuo-dao*, "Left Path" and described as *xie*, perverse or wrong, and *yao*, weird or heretical. Under constant threat of suppression, millenarians tended to form secret counter-communities, following their own leaders and codes of conduct, preserving and perpetuating their own heretical worldview.

Many, many times in East Asian history, when such millenarian groups judged that the coming of Maitreya was imminent or had already occurred among them, they launched uprisings against the rulers. Sometimes they held power in their home hills and valleys for a month or a season or half a year, sometimes they captured a few government strongholds or towns. As long as the ruling powers kept their cohesion, it was only a matter of time before they rallied superior military forces and defeated the rebels.

Millenarian Buddhism was particularly important in the fourteenth century, in T'aego's time, when millenarian Buddhists of the White Lotus religion in central China spearheaded the revolts that broke the Mongol empire in East Asia. In the 1350's millenarian groups came out in the open and took power over large regions of China. The Korean elite felt the shock of two invasions by millenarian armies into their territories. In moments of victory, in their zeal to sweep away the corruption of the passing age, and usher in the rule of Maitreya, the millenarian rebels made targets not only of the secular authorities and the landed upper class, but also of the wealthy Buddhist institutions and establishment monks and nuns.

KOREA AND EAST ASIA

All this only hints at the real richness and variety of the multicolored Buddhist spectrum in East Asia. Where do we find our buddha from Korea in all this? Where do we locate Korean Buddhism itself?

Korea: A thousand years of royal politics by T'aego's

time, rival tribes and confederations boiled down into three kingdoms and then into one; a rank-ridden society, dominated by nobles jealous of their pedigrees, nobles rich in lands and slaves, busy at court intrigue; different degrees of unfreedom for the subjugated majority, farmers and artisans bound to their occupations and localities and lords; heavy labor services, tax and rent in grain and cloth and local specialties; merchants tied to the lords, providing luxury imports to the elite of the capital.

Korea: A history of aristocratic warlord politics, infighting among the nobility, courtiers versus military commanders, centralizing monarch versus the aristocracy, strong kings and decadent kings, military strongmen behind the throne; periodic fragmentation under local lords, then relative unity reimposed by force; severe breakdowns of the ruling system, popular uprisings and new leaders coming to the fore, piecemeal emancipation for the lower orders, granted under duress.

Korea: Open borders to the wider world, ideas and techniques and people going back and forth; intimately linked to the neighboring forest peoples to the north; in the shadow of China, frequently borrowing, frequently bullied; linked by sea to the coastal world and the islands; forever faced with congeries of tribes and states mobilized for war, armed and dangerous; repeatedly invaded by Chinese, Khitan, Jurchen, Mongols, Japanese.

And some people imagine that old Asia was such a spiritual place.

Buddhism was not floating in a vacuum. In old Asia secular society with its chronic struggles and endemic injustice was not particularly "spiritual"; wisdom and compassion did not come easily. A realistic sense of the blood-and-guts history of old Asia helps us see Buddhism better for what it was. It awakens us to an appreciation of the true dimensions of the contribution of Buddhism (and Confucianism and Taoism) to humanizing civilized society in those lands.

Buddhism in Korea

Buddhist missionaries arrived in Korea in the fourth century C.E., bringing scriptures and images. By late in the century, Buddhism had been adopted by the royal houses of Koguryo and Paekche (two of the three Korean kingdoms), who saw in it a means of supernatural protection for their rule. Around 530, Buddhism was made the state religion of Silla (the third kingdom), which was then in the process of strengthening its central state and expanding its power and territory. The Korean elite became aware of texts like the *Benevolent King Sutra,* in which Buddha entrusts the care of the Dharma to the secular lords, and sets up a standard of virtuous rulership.

As in other Asian lands, in Korea, too, monarchs tried to tame the aristocracy and incorporate it into a unified royal state. They could draw a conceptual model from the Buddhist mandala, in which a central buddha is depicted surrounded by an orderly array of lesser figures. In the political analog, the monarch takes the place of the central buddha, and the regional political authorities are seen as the lesser emanations of the central power. By appearing as the chief patrons of the holy teaching, monarchs enhanced their own moral authority and universal claims. Kings would endow large temples set up in the centers of their rule, dedicated to the protection of the realm. Local temples would be designated as branch temples of the principal institutions and thus would be incorporated into a national system of allegiance and control.

By the 500's it appears Buddhism was firmly implanted in Korea. The first masterpieces of Korean Buddhist art date from this period: images of Shakyamuni Buddha and Maitreya Buddha carved into stone cliffs. There were Korean monks and nuns faithfully studying the *vinaya,* the codes of monastic discipline. Scholarly monks became experts in expounding the teachings of certain sutras. Even *hyangga,* the country people's chants and prayers for divine aid, began to take on Buddhist coloration. Concepts from Buddhist lore mixed with the native Northeast Asian tradition of shamanistic divining and healing.

The 600's were a period of intensive political and cultural contact between Korea and China. Korean monks traveled to China and made contact with the schools of Buddhist philosophy influential there, and returned to Korea as their representatives. Famous examples are Uisong, who received the teachings of the Huayan school, and Wonch'uk, whose concise summary of the Tiantai philosophy became a classic of East Asian Buddhism read through the ages. A few Korean monks, like their Chinese colleagues, even journeyed to India in search of sacred texts.

As a symbol of the multifaceted solidity of Korean Buddhism by this time, we have the figure of Wonhyo (617–686). Wonhyo wrote commentaries on many of the famous sutras and treatises. He also composed works to reconcile divergent interpretations of Buddhist philosophy and to refute one-sided partisan views. Wonhyo also is said to have traveled widely throughout Korea promoting Pure Land practices: Pure Land Buddhism was already becoming a widespread popular faith.

Silla

The seventh century was also a time of decisive political conflicts in Korea. China had been reunified around 580 under Emperor Wen of the Sui dynasty: a military aristocrat by birth, an astute warlord and dynastic politician, and a devoted patron of Buddhism. Unity in China usually signaled danger for Korea. Following the logic of second-generation inheritors needing new worlds to conquer, the second (and last) Sui emperor bankrupted the regime with his massive efforts around 610 to conquer Korea and add it to his domains. The northern Korean kingdom of Koguryo, hitherto the most powerful, bore the brunt of these Chinese invasions.

War in this period meant hungry armies with huge appetites for supplies and goods of all kinds: food, fuel, draft animals, fodder, leather, wood. War meant forced impressment of skilled artisans, wholesale coercion of labor to haul and carry and build fortifications, the seizure of women and girls and boys. Armies traveled with whole moving towns of camp-followers, baggage trains, and flocks.

War meant battlefield deaths, the slaughter of surrendered garrisons, hunting down stragglers after a rout, troops dying of disease in their camps; it meant plundered cities, rape, farms torn up and wells poisoned and orchards cut down, livestock animals slaughtered for meat and hides, people carried off into slavery or forced to become refugees. It was mass murder by blade and bludgeon and artificial famine: small in scale of course, compared to what our twentieth-century grandfathers and fathers achieved, and what we prepare for today, but the terror of its own time.

The Tang dynasty established its rule over China in the 620s; under the second-generation emperor in 645 came another invasion of Koguryo. Tang China was fully involved in the rivalries among the three Korean kingdoms, helping them attack each other, changing sides at its own convenience. But the southeastern Korean kingdom of Silla beat China at its own game in the peninsula. The rulers of Silla played off the Chinese menace against the other two kingdoms, and in the 660's Silla overthrew both its rivals with Chinese help. Silla moved to annex the territories of Koguryo and Paekche, and in 676 defeated a Chinese invasion force in central Korea to consolidate its authority. As they say in history books, Silla had "unified Korea."

This unity was only relative: battlefield victories and military supremacy still had to be translated into a ruling system, a system imposed on a pre-existing patchwork of local domains, power holders, and loyalties.

The Silla rulers proceeded in classical fashion dictated by the logic of circumstances. The country was held by a system of garrison units and mobile strategic forces of sworn followers. In the 680's a centralizing king ruthlessly curtailed the independence of the high nobility. The aristocrats of the conquered kingdoms were deported from their domains to five regional capitals, where they could be watched over, and in the longer run co-opted. Locally powerful families in the countryside had to send family members to serve at the capital, where they were hostages for the loyalty of their relatives back home.

The national territory was divided into nine regions, each with a governing bureau representing the central state. The leading partisans of the regime were rewarded from the large stock of land confiscated from conquered enemies: the Silla ruling house and top nobility became exceedingly rich. In the capital a National Confucian Academy was established, open to sons of the highest nobility, to educate them in the role of the loyal minister to the monarch.

Despite a veneer of Confucian ideas and Chinese bureaucratic forms, the top layers of society in Silla were deeply imbued with an aristocratic idea of politics. They firmly believed their superior descent gave them the right to the top positions of power in the state. Not that everyone agreed on which noble lines were the best: thus the ongoing struggle for power and honor was of vital concern. The leading contenders had armed retinues and vast landed wealth to back up their claims, besides connections by descent and marriage at court. But already in the seventh century the eminent Korean Confucian Kangsu took the Sage's teaching to its logical conclusion and advocated that talent and virtue should outweigh inherited rank when state offices were filled.

Society was structured around a hierarchy of statuses people were born into. Vast sections of the rural population were unfree, bound to the lands of wealthy nobles, overseen on the ground by a network of bailiffs and strong-arm collectors and village notables. Local groups of people were handed over along with the land they worked as grants to the nobility for service to the crown: in time these estates became hereditary possessions. Being a free peasant meant paying directly to the king's representatives, instead of to other lords. Villagers grouped behind their local elders, who were in charge of rendering submission to the higher authorities.

Upheaval was the main chance for social mobility, but most people dreaded upheaval, since they knew that mobility was more often downward than upward. Local classes of serfs and slaves sometimes rose up when pressed to the wall by extortionate demands or bad times. Sometimes they seized the change presented by open fighting among their social superiors to improve their lot. Only a handful of disgruntled nobles on the fringes of power or ambitious local strongmen and adventurers ever welcomed the prospect of political conflict. The worst fear of the free peasant, or even the tolerably situated serf, was to be driven from his home area by war or famine, and thus lose his place in the community, such as it was.

For most ordinary people, the best hope was that their masters would be humane enough to limit their exactions, and that they would live in a time of peace and relative prosperity. Then they could carry out their allotted roles with some predictability and security, and enjoy the domestic pleasures of having a family and seeing their descendants live on after them. They could express their nature in the narrow sphere of freedom left to them. This is where Buddhism opened other doors.

Confucian and Buddhist Influences

Against this menacing backdrop of military struggle and institutionalized oppression, both Confucian and Buddhist teachers were at work trying to promote more humane values in society. They tried to deflect people away from the norms of brute self-preservation and the war of all against all so prevalent all around them, away from the mentalities of subservience and resentment and displaced violence.

In Confucian eyes, social chaos and political strife are signs of dereliction of duty by the upper class. The top men have a duty to uphold proper values and serve as the moral leaders of society. At court they must serve the monarch as loyal ministers, unafraid to tell the truth. At home they should watch over the common people like benevolent parents, civilizing them and making them prosperous and content. If those in power exceed the proper limits, and abuse their authority for private gain, the result will be loss of the people's loyalty and inevitable disorder.

Like the other classical Chinese political philosophies, Confucianism taught that Heaven removes the mandate to rule from unfit leaders. Rulers who disrupt the moral unity of society by losing the people's support lose the mandate of Heaven. Conversely, political success comes to those who lead by moral force, by being properly aligned with the Heaven-endowed pattern, and thus winning the people's loyalty by serving their true interests.

If this sounds like empty moralizing today, so much the worse for us. As it happened, many of the most famous masters of *realpolitik* in East Asian history—the founders of the dynasties, the great unifiers and reunifiers, and the advisors and strategists around them—accepted this as hard fact, the basic axiom of politics.

When Buddhist teachers addressed emperors and kings in East Asia, they often exhorted them to live up to the example of the Confucian Sage Kings. The Sage Kings were creators of good order: they ruled by moral force, by winning people's hearts and minds. They were the legendary models of cultural creativity, public-mindedness, and impartiality. When the Sage Kings chose people to entrust power to, they always put ability and moral qualifications above hereditary claim.

Buddhism encountered deep social inequalities throughout old Asia, and Korea was no exception: everywhere there were long-established situations rooted in conquest and coercion, ethnic overlays, caste systems, all the long-cherished invidious distinctions humans revel in.

Maybe this is why all the great Buddhist teachers, from Shakyamuni Buddha himself up through the East Asian Zen and Pure Land masters, made it their business to associate with people in all walks of life, disregarding conventional social distinctions to appeal to them in terms of a universal enlightened nature inherent in all. The buddhas and bodhisattvas said so many things in so many ways to so many different people, covered the issue from so many angles, precisely so that they could communicate the "everywhere equal Dharma" in a world of self-defined, self-imposed diversity.

Buddhist philosophy, especially the perfection of wisdom literature, goes on at great length about the inherent equality of all phenomena, and the insubstantiality not only of social distinctions, but actually of all artificial distinctions. Ordinary humans are seen as trapped in a web of false distinctions: habitual opinions, skewed perceptions, arbitrary definitions, taboos, conventional roles. These generate more actions and more results, and become a self-perpetuating delusion that persists until death.

Buddhism is presented as a practical means to escape this trap, by refining away habitual false perceptions and uncovering other forms of perception that give access to wider realities. Meditation work is one part of doing this, but so are giving charity, keeping discipline, showing forbearance, marshaling energy, and developing wisdom, active wisdom in the world, where true discernment replaces false distinction-making. In Buddhism, "wisdom" is not the vague concept it is today. "Wisdom" means the wisdom of the buddhas: the great mirror wisdom, which encompasses all apparent phenomena as images in a mirror, the wisdom to know the inherent equality of all things, the wisdom of subtle observation, able to discern the real fabric of events, and the wisdom to carry out actions accordingly.

In its theory, Great Vehicle Buddhism goes beyond all mundane social distinctions: it teaches that everyone has buddha-nature, that all will eventually be saved. Classic Buddhist scriptures like the *Huayan Sutra* illustrate that enlightenment can be found up and down the range of social circumstances and "pure" and "impure" occupations. The great Pure Land teachers proclaimed their teaching open to all classes of people: invoking Amitabha was designed to be the simplest, most accessible gate to the Dharma. Zen teachers often made a point of disregarding social conventions, even the conventions of Buddhist formalists.

The most basic Zen stories flatly contradicted the conventional ideas that linked religious worth with social status or purity of descent. A pivotal figure in Zen lore, the grandfather of the great outward pulse in the 800's, was the sixth patriarch, Huineng of Caoqi (d. 714). Greatly revered in the Zen school, he was nevertheless traditionally presented as an illiterate aborigine, a woodcutter who awoke to the Dharma at once when he happened to hear the *Diamond Sutra* being recited in the marketplace where he was selling his wood. To tweak the local ethnocentrism, Zen teachers referred to the first patriarch of Zen, Bodhidharma, as the "red-bearded barbarian" or the "blue-eyed barbarian" and to Buddha himself as the "old barbarian."

But on the worldly scene, Buddhism certainly could not escape the social inequalities of old Asia or erase them. Buddhism was not a movement for democratic rule over society (for this was not seen as possible then), but it did foster small-scale relatively egalitarian groups operating here and there as autonomous entities. These could be groups with transcendental motives, as in the early Buddhist sangha of mendicants, or the self-supporting mountain communities of early Zen. Or they could be focused on the social side of religion, the community of fellow-believers who support each other through life's trials and share a distinctive group life, such as Pure Land and other devotional groups.

For the most part, in Korea and in the other Asian lands, Buddhism came to terms with the existing divisions in society, and institutionalized Buddhism inevitably came to reflect them. Monks with power in the long-established Buddhist institutions tended to come from privileged social backgrounds, from families accustomed to power and prestige. After all, it was the surrounding society the monks and nuns came from, within which the laity continued to live, that mainly shaped their attitudes.

Buddhist teachings could only redirect this to a limited extent. Buddhism could at best suggest an alternative source of authority, beyond the conventional judgments of society: namely, the deeds and words of the enlightened adepts. These might be men or women from any social background, any nationality: the only qualification was empowerment in the Dharma.

Korean Zen

Zen grew up as one of the periodic movements of renewal within Buddhism: an effort to turn away from routinized formalism and to reawaken to the original intent behind the teachings. First in China, then in Korea and Vietnam, and then in Japan, Zen teachers came on the scene to remind people to take Buddhism to heart, to make it their personal business, to follow the example of the buddhas and past masters and witness the reality of the Dharma.

The early Zen people moved around among the Buddhist communities of temples and monasteries, and networks of lay believers. Buddhist centers were home to a great diversity of monks and nuns pursuing various practices, ritual specialties, and branches of Buddhist learning. There was much ceremony, much catering to superstitious sensibilities. But there was also the tolerance to allow for a variety of approaches to Buddhism, from shallow to profound. Some of the early Zen teachers withdrew from the already established monasteries to set up new centers for those dedicated to a more rigorous concept of the monastic life. Groups of seekers would gather around an adept, drawn by his reputation for wisdom. Sometimes a Zen teacher became the most influential presence at an already established temple, which then became known as a Zen temple.

After several generations of widening transmission, Zen in China was well known as a distinctive style of Buddhism by the early 700's, when the empress Wu Zetian bestowed her patronage on Zen teachers in the imperial capitals of Chang'an and Luoyang. In the 800s Zen centers proliferated widely across China, and Vietnamese and Korean monks returning from China brought Zen to their homelands. The ninth and tenth centuries were the age when Zen became the intellectually predominant form of Buddhism in East Asia. Monumental works like the *Source Mirror* appeared, to show the fundamental harmony of Zen with the sutras and with philosophical Buddhism, to show the logic of the joint practice of Pure Land and Zen. The Zen masters whose sayings and doings became the classic public cases for twelfth- to sixteenth-century Zen were mostly people from the eight to the tenth centuries.

According to tradition, Zen got started in Korea through the works of a series of Korean masters who had studied for years with leading Zen teachers in China—in particular, the heirs of the great master Mazu (d. 788). From Chinese records and from travelers' reports, it appears that Korean monks were indeed relatively familiar visitors in Chinese temples, along with Japanese and South Asians and Central Asians. Zen sayings mention Silla and Champa (south of Vietnam) or Silla and Ferghana (west of the Tarim desert) as a metaphor for opposite ends of the world.

The Zen temples that made up the Silla dynasty's Nine Mountains system were founded in the ninth century; Precious Forest Temple, Porim-sa on Mount Kaji, Reality Temple, Silsang-sa, on Mount Silsang, Grand Peace Temple, T'ae-an-sa, on Mount Tongni, Steep Mountain Temple, Kulsan-sa, on Mount Sagul, Phoenix Forest Temple, Pongnim-sa, on Mount Pongnim, Flourishing Peace Temple, Hung-nyong-sa, on Lion Mountain, Phoenix Cliff Temple, Pongam-sa, on Mount Huiyang, Sages' Abode Temple, Songju-sa, on Mount Songju, and Vast Illumination Temple, Kwangjo-sa, on Mount Sumi. Though they attracted handsome patronage in their times, only four of these sites survive today.

More Korean Politics

The Zen school became established in Korea during the ninth century, a period when rivalries in the top layers of society were splitting the Silla ruling system apart. (Zen in China also became widely established during a period of militarism and disunity, ca. 750–960; likewise in Vietnam, ca. 900–1000, and Japan, ca. 1200–1350.)

At the Silla capital rival cliques of aristocrats struggled to control the throne and laid claims to royal blood. Leading nobles built up their own armed followings. This was the age of the castle-lords: strongmen who set themselves up in fortress-towns as independent rulers in their regions. Castle-lords along the coast were greatly enriched by their control of the brisk trade with China and Japan. In the last decade of the ninth century, there were widespread peasant revolts, and the Silla monarchy broke up: regional commanders built up their forces, proclaimed themselves kings and fought for supremacy. There was a generation of disunion and intermittent warfare, known in history books as the Later Three Kingdoms period.

A new unified dynasty emerged with the growing success of the military man Wang Kon, who rose from a mod-
est gentry background to become king of Later Koguryo,
and went on to proclaim himself king of Koryo in 918. By
935 Wang Kon had managed to defeat his main opponents
and to establish himself as paramount ruler in Korea. The
new Koryo state was a unified regime only relative to the
open warfare of the recent past. Many castle-lords still remained with independent power-bases intact, and Wang
Kon used marriage ties to form alliances with many of
them. Though he made sure to garrison the area of the old
Silla capital with troops loyal to himself, Wang Kon dealt
gently with the Silla nobility, and took a wife from the
deposed royal family of Silla, to lend his new regime some
of the aura of the old nobility.

By fits and starts a new ruling system was patched together, enabling the various layers of the elite to compose
their differences and share power. In tenth-century terms,
a unified state meant a state that sent out representatives
of the center to oversee the provinces, and at the same
time opened channels to co-opt the locally powerful into
state service. Compared with Silla, Koryo drew on a wider
aristocracy for its officials, although the nobles eligible
were still an exclusive group, registered separately from
other levels of the population. Despite partial, local gains
achieved under military pressure, the majority of the
population were still bound by their ascribed statuses:
some free peasants, many districts of unfree peasants, hereditary obligations on certain families to furnish soldiers
or low-level government minions.

Koryo Buddhism

Buddhism in many forms helped to console and instruct
people in Koryo in these years. There were many images
of Maitreya, the future buddha destined to bring peace
and harmony to the world. There were many images of
Vairocana, the Universal Illuminator, a buddha who rep-

resents the source of being, the universal reality pervading all things, a symbol of underlying coherence.

Wang Kon himself believed in Buddhism and attributed his success to it: he became the number-one patron in the land, by whose order many temples were built and many great ceremonies held. Many Koryo aristocrats built small private prayer temples in their compounds in the capital and on their country domains.

Buddhist temples were classified according to whether their inmates specialized in Son, that is, Zen, or Kyo, the scriptural teachings, the sutras and philosophical texts. There were pious donors to pay for very ornate copies of the scriptures on fine paper. Lay people often hired monks and nuns to chant sutras, and this, along with performing rituals, was the main religious focus (and chief means of making a living) for many monks and nuns. The Nine Mountains Zen temples attracted patronage from local high society, and became established institutions. Many stupas were erected to the memory of deceased Zen teachers. There were nobles who became monks and nuns and donated part of their property to the temples where they intended to reside. Buddhist establishments thus acquired large possessions and ties to the aristocracy.

The ritual calendar emphasized the links between Buddhism and the Koryo state. Twice a year there were great ceremonies invoking the supernatural aid of the buddhas and bodhisattvas, as well as native deities, for the protection of the realm. The birthdays of the reigning king and his predecessor were celebrated with large assemblies and open vegetarian feasts. There were public gatherings to recite the *Benevolent King Sutra* and to pray for social peace. On the fifteenth day of the sixth (lunar) month, rites were held to commemorate the king's vow to be a bodhisattva. Buddha's birthday was celebrated on the eighth day of the fourth month. Prayers to ease the karmic burdens of the dead were recited at assemblies on the fifteenth day of the seventh month.

For most Koreans of all ranks, these great ceremonies were one familiar face of Buddhism. Temples were known for the opulence of their buildings and statues, the splendor of ceremonies and festivals, and for the number of monks and nuns they could assemble for grand displays.

The Koryo elite became fascinated with Song Chinese high culture. Contemporary China was in the midst of a great self-conscious florescence of culture. New styles in art, literature, political thought, and philosophy grew out of a new awareness of the ancient cultural legacy. In Korea, Vietnam, and Japan, gentlemen with the wealth and leisure to pursue cultural interests turned to Song Chinese models. From the 1000's through the 1200's, Buddhist and Confucian ideas acquired new impetus in all these countries.

The internationalism of Zen was ensured through person-to-person contacts and exchanges, and wide circulation of important writings. If we read famous Zen texts from the 1200's from China, Korea, Vietnam, and Japan, the deep unity of intent and vision stands out above the local differences of idiom and emphasis. *Chan* in China, *Son* in Korea, *Thien* in Vietnam, *Zen* in Japan—the local language varied, but not the message. There was a common stock of Zen lore which Zen teachers in all these countries knew.

Where the Zen masters differed was not on matters of principle, but in what particular materials they utilized in their practical teachings. Some stressed certain Zen devices, some stressed other Buddhist methods like reciting the buddha-name or chanting spells or doing visualizations. Some made frequent use of Buddhist analytical categories and the detailed meditation perspectives contained in the various sutras, methods of disassembling and redirecting conscious experience. Some emphasized esoteric styles of companionship, other stressed various forms of community service. Some employed physical exercises and Taoist forms of energy work, the East Asian analogs of yoga. Even local folk religion with its spirits and power places figured in the teachings of Zen masters. In light of the principle of skill in means, such diversity was considered natural and proper to the true teaching. The unifying factor was the intent.

Given the interchanges between East Asian Buddhist communities in this period, it comes as no surprise that there are parallels between the works of leading Buddhists in Koryo Korea and Song China. Certain landmarks are easy to see that suggest the scope of Buddhism in Koryo.

In 1087, under royal patronage, a complete set of wooden printing blocks was cut for the whole Buddhist canon. Down through East Asian history, an enormous range of Buddhist materials was assembled and preserved by efforts like this, including both translations of ancient Indian scriptures and works composed in East Asia. Sets of the canon were always among the prized possessions of leading Buddhist temples and monasteries.

The Koryo monk Uich'on (1055–1101, fourth son of King Munjong) studied intensively in China and returned home to establish a Korean Ch'ont'ae school, based on the Chinese Buddhist Tiantai philosophy. This school gives a systematic account that categorizes the scriptural teachings and the meditations rooted in them into several patterns, and then reflects the patterns into each other. Its schemes are both conceptually clear and comprehensive, and oriented toward actual practice.

The great Son master Chinul (1158–1210) founded his Chogye school (named after the abode of the sixth patriarch of Zen: Caoqi in Chinese, Chogye in Korean) in order to reunify the various Korean Son schools. As many Chinese adepts had done, in his writings Chinul reemphasized the underlying harmony between Zen and the scriptural teachings. He stressed that abstruse talk was no substitute for solid experience of reality. Chinul's work was powerfully continued by his disciple Chin'gak Hyesim (1178–1234). From the writings of these two men it is clear that these masters of Son in Korea had full access to the treasury of scriptural and Zen Buddhist lore known to their peers in other East Asian lands.

In the realm of Buddhist history, the Koryo monk Kakhun put together a collection of biographies of eminent Korean monks that appeared in 1215, modeled on the assembled biographies of monks that were an important part of Buddhist literature in China.

In belles-lettres, the Son monk Iryon (1206–1289) wrote a work, *Stories of the Three Kingdoms,* which fleshed out the histories of the ancient Korean kingdoms with personalized drama, fables, and folklore. Again, there was a Chinese book with the same title, romanticizing a period in Chinese history.

Koryo: Confucianism and Power Politics

Even as Buddhism flourished, Confucianism gained ground in Koryo too. Tenth-century Korean Confucians advocated that positions in the state be filled on criteria of merit and ability, not by right of descent. The regime set up an examination system in 958, which allowed educated sons of good families to gain entry to government office by passing exams in literary composition or the classics or a combination of literary classics and institutional history.

Success in the examinations demanded years of preparation and extensive rote memorizing. Competition was keen because success brought honor for one's family and the opportunities for wealth and power open to officials. Since the (Chinese) classics that made up the curriculum were saturated with Confucian perspectives, the examination system gave well-off families a practical motive to have their sons indoctrinated in Confucianism.

Critics in China often pointed out that more suitable men would be chosen as officials if the examinations tested for practical knowledge of administration and statecraft, rather than for rote memory and ability to string together phrases. Certainly the examination system did not make officialdom purely a career-open-to-talent. Women were categorically excluded. Only the more prosperous families could afford the years of education their sons would need to compete successfully. Moreover, in Koryo as in Song China itself, high officials had the right to extend "protection" to one or more of their kinsmen, automatically conferring on them official rank and bypassing the examination system.

In the eleventh century there were many private Confucian academies founded in Koryo to teach the sons of the nobility. Schools founded by high officials and scholars eclipsed the old National Academy as centers of Confucian learning. The Koryo aristocracy must have gained in national consciousness through its exposure to Confucian political education, which stresses the duty of the elite to be moral leaders of society, and prescribes for the elite man the ideal role of loyal minister to the monarch.

Despite the examination system and the best advice of Confucians, the Koryo state remained staunchly aristocratic. The key men in the state owed their positions above all to family connections, and to their prowess at intrigue and warfare. Politics was dominated by the personal ambitions of aristocrats unwilling to yield pride of place to each other. For most of these men, state office was not considered a public trust so much as a private possession, an honor due high birth, or something won in war.

Thus it comes as no surprise that Koryo unraveled along lines similar to Silla earlier. For three generations in the tenth century, the centralizing dynasty fought a mostly successful battle to incorporate the whole country under its rule and to tame entrenched local strongmen and old families. Then in the eleventh century supreme power passed to other top noble clans that had married into the royal house, who ruled in the name of the king. Rivalries intensified within the top nobility maneuvering for position around the throne.

Koryo was also exposed to foreign dangers. Internal divisions within the Korean elite invited foreign intervention. The Khitan kingdom that ruled in Manchuria put heavy military pressure on Koryo (but also kept Song China in check). From about 990 to 1020, Korea suffered three major Khitan invasions. In the 1030's the Koryo rulers oversaw the building of a defensive wall across the peninsula to ward off the Khitan raiders. A precarious truce prevailed along this armed border.

Late in the eleventh century, a new tribal confederation ruled by the nobility of the Jurchen people rose to power beyond the Khitan. After defeating the Khitan, and absorbing many of their subject peoples, the Jurchen achieved a stunning victory over the Song empire, and occupied North China in the 1120's. Koryo was forced to acknowledge the overlordship of the Jurchen, who called their state the Jin dynasty. This humbling of the Koryo state's power opened the way for even deeper conflict within the Koryo nobility, who armed against each other and consolidated regional bases.

The nobility were stymied by an age-old dilemma. If the central power got too strong, it could interfere in their local prerogatives and claim too big a share of the local revenues and labor power. If the central power got too weak, the country could be overwhelmed by foreign invaders. When the central power began to slip, the magnates had every opportunity and incentive to build up their own followings and independent power-bases, and this in turn weakened the central state further.

This downward spiral took place in twelfth-century Koryo. One climax came in 1170 with a great massacre of the capital nobility, who were the civilian officials of the state, by rebellious military commanders from the provinces. The lands and slaves of the capital aristocrats were taken over by military officers. For the next generation there was a succession of generals who succeeded each other by assassination and coup d'état. Throughout the country, military leaders created private armies and ruled supreme in their home areas. Even Buddhist monasteries armed themselves to defend their holdings. There were rebellions of serfs in the countryside and slave uprisings in the towns. According to a famous anecdote, the spokesman for the rebel slaves in the capital in 1198 openly rejected the idea that only aristocrats were qualified to rule: recent history proved, he declared, that even the lowly could rise to command.

Once again a semblance of political unity was restored with the emergence of a paramount military chief, Ch'oe Ch'unghon. The new ruler gradually multiplied his forces and put in place representatives of his own regime to intervene strategically in local politics and to rein in powerful families. Like the shoguns in Japan, Ch'oe kept the old royal family on the throne as his puppets. Rival aristocrats were made vassals or else destroyed. Rebel chieftains too strong to defeat were co-opted into the regime as local bosses. To allay discontent and placate rebels, many unfree people were granted ordinary commoner status.

The Ch'oe regime had barely a generation to solidify before it was overtaken by a new catastrophe, the Mongol invasions. The world-conquering Mongol organization was dedicated in 1206: within two decades the Mongols dominated North and Central Asia, and were poised to take North China and Iran.

After years of growing menace, during which the Mongols smashed the Jurchen state in Manchuria and began to demand tribute from Koryo, Mongol forces crossed into Korea in 1231. The court nobility abandoned the capital the next year and took refuge from the invaders on an offshore island. For four decades the court elite abdicated political leadership and lived a isolated life of dwindling luxury, while six Mongol invasions thoroughly devastated the valleys that contained most of Korea's arable land and people. Finally a faction gained ascendancy that overthrew the Ch'oe and made peace with the Mongols: in 1270 what remained of the old court nobility returned to the traditional Koryo capital at Kaesong and accepted Mongol rule. The remnants of the Ch'oe forces were wiped out in the bases they had established along the south coast.

THE MONGOL PERIOD

By the second half of the thirteenth century, the Mongol overlords had evolved from the raid-and-plunder mentality of their early conquests, and had come to know the advantages of settled rule, taxation, and tribute, and the pleasures of living as an upper class. After much uncertainty and travail, the conquered societies had managed to come to terms with the new masters.

State and Society

Despite its veneer of Chinese bureaucratic forms, the Mongol regime in East Asia, called the Yuan dynasty, still remained military in substance and tone. It was not a tightly centralized state, but more a league of raiding parties that had come to stay, all theoretically subordinate to a paramount chief, the great khan. Multiethnic armies commanded by Mongol nobles established themselves as regional authorities, and if need be cooperated militarily against common enemies. In their own areas they drew labor services and supplies and taxes in kind from the people as they saw fit, and were free to apportion lands and serfs as fiefs for their own leading officers. The various Mongol regional commanders were linked to each other by blood connections or inherited sworn allegiances tracing back to the conquest.

Three Mongol commanderies were established in Korea: in the northwest, in the northeast, and along the south coast. Korea as a whole was included in the territory of the "Area Government for Conquering the East" and was the major base for the Mongol invasions of Japan in 1274 and 1281. The Koryo royal family were required to marry into the Mongol ruling house of Qubilai Khan, and became subservient vassals. Intrigues among Mongol grandees and their collaborators determined the choice of royal heirs, and led to reigning kings being deposed and replaced. The Koryo crown prince had to reside in the Mongol capital, as hostage for the Koryo king's obedience.

The Mongol elite were thoroughly convinced of their own superiority, and confident that Heaven had granted them dominion over the world. They classified their subject peoples by ethnic and occupational categories, and assigned obligations accordingly. As they saw it, conquest gave them the right to live off the conquered peoples and to take whatever they wanted from them: grain, silver, luxury textiles, boys and girls to be slaves, artisans to staff their armories and workshops. Even as the rulers of a vast diverse empire, the Mongols held to the old tribal ideal of a society held together by bonds of personal fealty and direct subjugation. An elite nobility of the khan's "companions" held the leading positions in the state, acted as the commanders of the Mongol military network, and wielded supreme civil and military power.

In Korea the Mongols ruled through seventy to eighty collaborator grandees, some of noble stock of varying degrees of antiquity, some military parvenus. Residing at the capital, these great nobles used their power to amass vast holdings in lands and slaves and to collect their own revenues. Alongside the Mongol garrison establishments, these grandees were the actual rulers of the land and people of Korea. Each stood at the apex of a network of lesser lords and assignees and bailiff-strongmen overseeing their possessions for them, while they struggled to defend or build up their political standing in the capital.

The upward-looking, inward-looking high elite could not help but be relatively out of touch with local society, from which they drew their wealth, and which they ruled at a distance. When the central power slipped, high position in the state was no longer effective as the high nobility's trump card. Real power tended to devolve into the grasping hands of strongmen on the scene: then the high nobility often found that they needed their bailiffs more than their bailiffs needed them. When the state became militarily too weak for its role as ultimate guarantor of the social order, then the local power-holders would begin to see to their own interests first, to keep local resources for themselves, and to solidify their independent local power.

The Mongols' relative newness to the values of the civilizations they conquered left them room to be very eclectic in their choices of whom and what to patronize. From the viewpoint of the previous elites of the conquered countries, the Mongol rule was a period of upstarts and of disconcerting changes in fashion and taste. New styles of painting and of drama took hold. Certain Mongol words and styles of dress came into use. The Mongols brought in foreigners as high officials and sometimes elevated local henchmen who could never have risen to power under the old order. For a lion's share of the profits, Mongol nobles invested in and extended political protection to certain merchant associations made up mostly of Central Asians. These operated in many markets across the Mongol domain and linked East Asia more intensely than ever before with Central Asia and the Muslim world.

For religious institutions anxious to protect their possession, there was a scramble to be sanctioned by the new rulers and to attract their patronage. Buddhists, Taoists and Confucians (not to mention Muslims, Christians, Zoroastrians and sundry others) all offered their teachings to the new rulers. Some approached the new masters with self-seeking motives; others as a community service, to influence the Mongols toward more humane values.

Religion in the Mongol Period

Taoism easily survived the Mongol onslaught: it had the strength of its diffuse organization, and its veils of folklore and illusion to beguile the conquerors. The lore of the

Taoist inner adepts was as alive as ever, now in its long dialogue with Zen. Popular Taoism was resilient, hydra-headed. Shrines marking local deities and power places could be looted and temporarily disrupted, but popular belief and devotional practices would recreate them before long. The Mongol conquerors soon came to feel for the sanctity of these things: the popular image of the Taoist adept as uncanny sorcerer was not entirely foreign to the Mongols, who had their own tradition of shamans and trance.

Confucianism held on through the Mongol conquest in private Confucian academies that persisted wherever local landed society reestablished some stability under the new overlords. At first the conquest shut the Confucians out of their traditional roles as political advisors to the monarch and as members of the state bureaucracy. Confucian thinkers concentrated on maintaining the purity of cultural norms in the private sphere of the gentry's family life, and on reasserting Confucian values in local community leadership.

When the grandsons and great-grandsons of the Great Khan got around to adopting Chinese state forms for the Yuan dynasty, Confucianism was accorded a more prominent place. Still keeping most military-executive power in Mongol hands, the regime allowed for some offices to be filled via an examination system. The Cheng-Zhu school of Confucianism became the standard of orthodoxy in the examinations in 1313 (though the Song dynasty philosophers Cheng Hao, Cheng Yi, and Zhu Xi would have been aghast at the Yuan dynasty).

This Confucian orthodoxy solidified around the idea that Confucian social norms are an inherent part of the pattern of reality, and the only possible basis for civilized government and cultured personalities. Buddhism was strenuously rejected by this school for being unworldly, amoral, and of foreign origin. Even though many of these Confucians spent significant amounts of time in quiet meditation and inward contemplation, in their stated philosophy they insisted that Buddhism and Confucianism have nothing in common. They spoke against other Confucians who admitted openness to Buddhist ideas and who freely drew parallels between the two religions.

Buddhism evolved in many directions in Mongol-dominated East Asia. During the initial period of invasion and conquest, Buddhist temples as centers of accumulated wealth and finery presented obvious targets for plundering armies. Temples were looted and burned and monastic communities scattered. Only masters greatly renowned for holiness stood a chance of turning aside the conquerors' war-parties by their power to inspire awe. Other perceptive religious leaders organized retreats when disaster was inevitable, or provided shelter for people in flight, saving what could be saved.

A exemplary figure in the first generation of the Mongol conquest was the Buddhist layman Yelu Chucai, a high noble in the Jin dynasty, who was also an advanced student of the foremost Zen teacher in North China at the time, Wansong. Impressing the Great Khan by his loyalty to his fallen master, the deposed Jin emperor, Yelu Chucai became a trusted political advisor, who worked to educate the Mongol chiefs in less destructive forms of exploitation. Skillful means in this case meant convincing the Mongols that there was a limit to what could be taken from the people at any one time, that it would be more profitable to rule and tax agriculture than to destroy it.

As the Mongols established their permanent rule and learned more of the conquered peoples' institutions and beliefs, they were more and more exposed to religious attitudes current among the people they now ruled over. The headquarters of the Mongol leaders were host to a multitude of religious delegations and holy men. Some came to press their claims to sanctity and to try to convert the Mongol nobles to their doctrines. Many came seeking the khan's protection for their institutions, to confirm their right to exist and keep their holdings. Some religious teachers even came to court on the most dangerous, delicate mission of all: to get the ear of the lord and dissuade him from tyranny.

As they swept across the heart of the old world, the Mongol nobility and their retainers were exposed to diverse forms of Buddhism in North China, Korea, South China, and Tibet, to Islam and Nestorian Christianity in Central Asia and Iran, and to Taoism and Confucianism in East Asia. In the first generation of conquest, there were seeming anomalies, like Christian Mongol nobles in China, or Buddhist Mongol lords in Iran, but over time most Mongols turned to variants of the "world religion" of the regions they ruled: Buddhism in East Asia, Islam elsewhere.

In its third generation, during the second half of the 1200's, the Mongol "world empire" divided into four regional zones (East Asia, Central Asia, Iran and the Middle East, the Pontic steppe). The Mongols ruling East Asia took up Chinese imperial forms and became the Yuan empire.

As befitted the ruler of "all under Heaven," the Yuan emperor became the most munificent patron of Buddhism, Taoism, and Confucianism. Many Taoist and Buddhist temples received imperial patronage. There were funds for local Confucian schools, and as the Mongol regime became more sinicized, Confucian advisors began to figure at court. Many Buddhist and Taoist temples were specially dedicated to the protection of the state and the longevity of the ruler, and many monks and nuns were employed in the endless succession of rituals.

Tantra

It was Tantric Buddhism in Tibetan form that found particular favor with Mongol patrons. In the seventh, eighth, and ninth centuries, Tantric Buddhism flashed

52

across Asia: from India to Southeast Asia and Java, from India to Tibet and Central Asia, and by both routes to China and Korea and Japan. In this first pulse, Tantric images and chants and ritual procedures left their mark on Buddhism in countries like Korea and Japan and Tibet. In these lands Tantra countered well-established native traditions of magic by displaying formidable esoteric powers of its own. The arresting images and sounds of Tantra played an important role in the early propagation of Buddhism in these countries. Through ritual and art, Tantra managed to attract attention among the nobility and penetrated their stylized little worlds of blood and honor with new concepts and orientations.

Tantra advanced its practical methods from the principle that the apparent world, the web of energy and matter, is an expression of the absolute reality. Higher states are achieved by aligning the seeker properly with certain arrays of color and sound and imagery. Tantric initiates learned to visualize intricate mandalas showing the cosmos as a complex of many levels of apparent realities and higher powers. Wisdom and compassion and the various mystic powers were personified as "deities" and depicted in religious art. Tantric practitioners enacted complicated rituals in which they identified with these personified forces and through them merged with and reenacted the cosmic process.

Tantra is best known for its elaborate rituals, its mantras, and its psychedelic art: these are its special peaks. But Tantric adepts in Tibet and elsewhere were fully conversant with the whole heritage of Buddhist sutras and philosophical classics. They began their religious lives with years and decades of basic Buddhist practices before moving on to Tantric studies. Because its colorful rites and antinomian practices could easily be misused for sensual or emotional purposes, Tantra was always an esoteric tradition, whose full secrets were only revealed to initiates who had undergone a long process of purification and dedications.

Mongol patronage gave Tantric Buddhism a new prevalence in East Asia. Tibetan lamas and Tibetan-style temples were established in many centers of Mongol rule. At public ceremonies patronized by the Mongol grandees, people could see ritual implements and attire and altar design and images in the Tibetan Tantric style. Many East Asian popular Buddhist rituals came to incorporate long intricate chants in the Tantric manner. The super-ornate temple facades and gaudy, crowded altars seen in later East Asian Buddhist and Taoist temples may be another reflection of this Tantric infusion.

Pure Land and Other Lay Devotionalism

Pure Land devotionalism was already on the upsurge prior to the Mongol eruption. The strain of militarization and heightened warfare was being felt in China, Korea, and Japan throughout the twelfth and thirteenth centuries. If prospects in this world seemed hopeless, if the weight of accumulated evil seemed too heavy and moral compromise was the price of survival, Pure Land Buddhism still offered salvation to anyone who invoked the name of Amitabha with faith. No longer dependent on their own feeble powers, Pure Land believers could trust in Amitabha to grant them rebirth in his paradise.

Even on the most mundane levels, membership in a Pure Land association brought tangible benefits: a community of fellow-believers who could be relied on for aid and comfort, the feeling of belonging somewhere. Pure Land members also gained by encouraging each other in the simple but effective practice of reciting the buddha-name, creating a mood of calm focus in place of anxiety and dread or aimless malaise.

On a continuum with the Pure Land groups were other associations of lay people dedicated to living a pure and simple Buddhist life. People wanted to assure their karmic prospects through strict adherence to Buddhist norms. These groups existed in many varieties under a wide range of names: the original White Lotus Society founded in twelfth-century China was one of them. (Later the term "White Lotus religion" was applied generically to a whole range of popular Buddhist groups, including millenarians.)

Demanding a return to the original inspiration of Buddhism, groups in this trend often took on an anticlerical cast. They condemned the Buddhist establishment for succumbing to luxury and greed. These lay groups defined themselves in contrast to the corrupt clergy, as strict vegetarians who did not break the prohibitions on alcohol and sexual excess laid down by Buddha. They repudiated selfish gain, valued frugality, and practiced mutual aid. They thought that sincere people in lay life could fulfill the Buddhist Path themselves, without the guidance of spurious monks and nuns. The stress was on strict adherence to the norms of one's own religious group, often reinforced by regular public confession in front of the community.

Though strict moralists in their own minds, these groups were regularly accused of immorality. Why? Because they held meetings attended by both men and women, and sometimes allowed women to rise to leadership roles. "Meeting by night, dispersing at dawn, men and women mingling together indiscriminately"—this was one of the standard phrases official society used when condemning popular religious groups as heterodox. For women of independent and unconventional personalities in old Asia, one of the few ways they could come to the fore in a wider community outside the home was as teachers and cult leaders and mediums in popular religious groups.

Many of these groups had on hand their own scriptures: books in the style of the sutras, which reworked the Great Vehicle Buddhist message to address the needs of their communities. Sectarian texts usually stressed a few main points, giving both practical techniques and an overall worldview justifying the revelations of their founders. Some sectarian scriptures had millenarian themes and prophesied a new era to come, sustaining the hopes of the communities of believers. But the authorities looked on such tracts as heretical and subversive, and it was often extremely dangerous to be discovered in possession of them.

Heretical or not, popular religious communities survived not just on belief and myth, not only on mutual aid pacts and community feeling. They also offered their followers specific spiritual and physical techniques and courses of practice. Some groups practiced faith-healing and the use of protective charms. Some teachers were herbalists and curers and made appeal to nature spirits. Some stressed techniques of energy circulation and therapeutic exercise and massage akin to Taoist practices. Some groups set up networks of overnight lodges and other amenities for people in traveling occupations. Many groups simply met to chant their own scriptures and to strengthen their minds in that fashion. They tended and embellished their shrines and halls, passed down their beliefs to their children, and marked time with their own ritual and cosmic calendar.

Legend and relative chronology suggest that the now world-famous techniques of unarmed combat and other martial arts also developed out of this milieu. Heterodox groups under the threat of suppression had a good motive for learning self-defense, and physical energy-work could be developed in this direction. According to legend, the martial arts began when a group of monks-of-the-people banded together and vowed militant resistance against the overpowering injustice of the age.

Millenarian Beliefs

The ago-old millenarian stream in popular Buddhism came to the fore again under Mongol rule. From now on the "White Lotus religion" was the catch-all term used in the official histories for any of the millenarian groups predicting the coming of Maitreya and a new era (symbolized by the color white). The Yuan government issued legal prohibitions against the White Lotus religion in 1281, 1303, and, after allowing a decade of legality, again in 1322.

Wherever possible, the authorities searched out and destroyed White Lotus temples, along with their images and scriptures. But the Yuan regime was not more successful than the Song in rooting out heretical groups. Heterodox groups could shift names and forms, and hide behind innocuous facades. This made it hard for the authorities to distinguish them from obedient(and hence legally and customarily tolerated) religious associations.

There was also the material and mental impact of the Mongol conquest. By setting aside the established rulers, erratically imposing a new system of domination, and unpredictably intensifying the rate of exploitation, the Mongols broke open social space for the millenarian groups to spread and solidify.

After preparing for many years in secret, in the 1350's White Lotus groups all across central China rose in arms against the Yuan regime. While a loose network of Yuan commanderies held out in certain cities, and gentry-led militia protected the large property-holders in some locales, broad areas of the country came under control of regimes derived form millenarian movements. Many wealthy temples were plundered and their monks defrocked and driven off. Many of the landed class fled the onslaught of the millenarian armies, and for the time being lost their possessions.

The fighting dragged on in a many-cornered struggle through the 1350's and 1360's: millenarian against rival millenarian against Mongol remnants and their Chinese and other collaborators. Millenarian armies fighting against the Mongols in northeast China marched into Korea in 1359 and 1362, to the consternation of elite society there. The more zones rebels became active in, the more the remaining Yuan forces became isolated in defensive positions, concerned only to preserve their remaining bases.

Over the course of the protracted warfare, within the millenarian ranks men more concerned with the mechanics of power came to the fore. Ambitious warchiefs began to see the logic of cooperating with the previously established locally influential big families: when it came to drawing resources from society to build military power, in newly annexed areas it was far easier to tax and rule the pre-existing social order, than to put everything up for grabs by a leveling social revolution and disrupt the customary extraction of a surplus. Initially, millenarian believers were concentrated in certain locales where they first took power: in these limited zones a new millenarian-defined social order existed for a time. But when these rebel centers became in turn the nuclei of regional statelets and extended rebel rule far and wide, even where they could link up with pre-existing clandestine sympathizers, over such a wide territory real millenarian believers were bound to be a minority.

Though millenarian revolts played a crucial part in overthrowing the Mongol regime in China, their struggles did not usher in the Maitreyan age. As ultimate victory came within his grasp, Zhu Yuanzhang, the peasant-born founder of the new Ming dynasty, found it politic to disavow his own millenarian background. Once in power, he denounced and once again outlawed the White Lotus religion and all its offshoots. Groups that persisted in their beliefs in the coming of Maitreya were denounced as a threat to good order and, wherever possible, broken up by force. The millenarian tradition went underground again.

We have a report on these upheavals by one of T'aego's exact contemporaries in the Zen school; Chushi (1298–1369) was a leading Zen master in South China during the last decades of the Yuan dynasty, a famous teacher whose congregation included Chinese gentlemen, Koreans, and Japanese. Explaining the recent disasters to some monks, Chushi said:

When the times are like these, where should brothers who are intent on the Path put down their bundles?

What have all Buddhist teaching centers up to now been founded for?

So that you and a few of your hometown "companions in the Dharma" can make plans for your bellies and foster your ignorance? So that you can form groups and create hellish karma?

If you push the Buddha Dharma and Zen Path off to one side, don't you know that when the results of your actions arrive, you won't be able to escape? Nobody will take your place among the torments of hell!

These days since the outbreak of the fighting, in general hardly any of the large, officially recognized temples remain. Why are things like this?

Because the string of evil is full and the fruits of karma are ripe. All this is self-made, self-received. Who else would you have take the blame?

When the buddhas and Zen masters admonished you to leave home, it was not to be for the sake of food and clothing and reputation and profit. It was for the sake of the great affair of birth and death, because impermanence is swift.

Seek out enlightened teachers and visit spiritual friends: study earnestly until you understand clearly. With a burst of power, you will become a buddha. Then you can repay the profound benevolence of your parents, and save the world's people. If you are not like this, then why have you left home?

Zen in Mongol Times

Zen as an institutional presence could not escape the turmoil of the Mongol domination. During the first generation of Mongol invasions of North China and Korea from 1230 to the 1250's, Zen establishments suffered along with other Buddhist and Taoist temples and shrines. Fleeing monks and nuns had to scatter among the people, and many lost their institutional niches.

So heavy was the destruction in Korea that only very fragmentary records remain of the leading Korean Buddhist teachers between Chin'gak (d. 1234) and T'aego (fl. 1340–1381). Temples with the worldly sense to have armed themselves, of course, just became special targets of Mongol military efforts. In general, accumulated wealth was plundered, revenue-producing possessions were confiscated, donors lost their positions and fled, congregations of monks and nuns were dispersed or taken into captivity.

Another generation went by before the Mongol conquest of South China (ca. 1279). During this time the Mongols acquired some respect for the holiness of Buddhism, as well as a knowledge of Chinese methods of rule. The large concentration of Zen centers in southeast China was spared wanton destruction. Like the Southern Song realm as a whole, it was captured relatively intact by Qubilai's grand offensive (which enveloped South China from northeast, northwest and southwest at once). Zen travelers in the thirteen and fourteenth centuries continued to move back and forth between China and Korea, Japan, and Vietnam: seaborne communication and travel reached a new peak.

The main trends that were to be characteristic of Zen in the Yuan period were already apparent before the coming of the Mongols, and probably owe more to endogenous factors in Buddhist history than to the conquest itself.

Already by the year 1200 Zen literature had grown very intricate. The sayings and doings of the earlier masters had become "public cases" for meditation and study, and there were many famous collections in circulation that assembled sets of cases along with pointers, commentaries, verses, abrupt comments, and even comments on famous previous comments. The striking originality and variety of mood and metaphor and layered depths of meaning found in this literature had duly impressed high culture. But some people mistook the beauty and subtlety for the thing itself, and reveled in sheer complexity and "adding frost to snow." In this way the tradition of public cases and meditation on Zen sayings became ever more self-referential and deeply embedded in layers of commentary.

When Zen styles of expression were pursued for aesthetic reasons, as styles, or as intellectual playthings, aiming for novelty and shock value per se, the original intent and religious effectiveness were lost. Zen adepts often reproached their contemporaries for "lip-service Zen." They mocked self-styled teachers and seekers who bandied about Zen phrases meaninglessly in an attempt to create an air of wisdom and mystery. Memorizing sayings, vying to coin new metaphors, mechanically applying fragments of classic methods, phony teachers and students unable to tell the difference unwittingly undermined Zen with pseudo-Zen. Whenever Zen had an established place in society and a routinized image in culture, this type of degeneration was always possible.

How did the genuine teachers adapt to this situation? They reemphasized the practical orientation of Zen. The classic Zen manuals of discipline were printed and widely circulated. Zen teachers again stressed the complementarity of Zen and the scriptural teachings. They told their listeners that to attempt to study Zen without knowing the sutras and Buddhist philosophy was as futile as trying to learn how to run before knowing how to crawl.

One method that became more and more prevalent was to integrate Pure Land practice into the Zen outlook. Zen teachers recommend buddha-name recitation to enable people to become mindful of buddha. With the mind focused through the sound of the buddha-name, extraneous mental activities, cares and woes and idle hopes all recede. The "Pure Land" is the purity of inherent mind, our buddha-nature. It comes into view when the everyday habitual mind is quieted and purified through buddha-name recitation.

Zen teachers stressed that Pure Land methods had to be followed with dedicated intent and without interruption. According to them, admixture of wandering, grasping, impure thoughts would block the effectiveness of reciting the buddha-name. The goal of reciting the buddha-name was sustained buddha-remembrance: mindfulness of buddha, which is a remembering of our true identity. "The Pure Land is the pure land of inherent mind, Amitabha Buddha is the inherent enlightened nature of mind."

Another Zen-style adaptation of Pure Land practice was this: after learning how to invoke Amitabha steadily, the person intently reciting the buddha-name contemplates the question, Who is the one reciting the buddha-name? This became one of the widely used public cases of Yuan times, symbolizing the linking of Zen and Pure Land.

Yuan period Zen masters repudiated the lip-service Zen they saw around them, but they had no reason to reject the rich bequest of verbal teachings they inherited from their predecessors. They pointed out that genuine Zen sayings were not random creations, but reflected the logic of the enterprise of enlightenment already depicted in the sutras. It was to be expected that good teachings would be misapplied, and that spurious imitations would arise. They continued the old tradition of Zen talk themselves, but they knew that Zen utterances could only come from real experience: anything less would be an obvious fabrication to the enlightened eye.

Yuan period Zen teachers redirected attention back to the example of their earlier masters, to the intent behind the striking phrases. They found their audiences' "knowledge of Zen" had already become a mass of clichés that was freezing and blocking them. So the adepts of the period specialized in demolishing standard interpretations and using classic sayings "upside-down and sideways." They teased those self-styled Zen experts who had a seemingly solid command of verbal knowledge, but who were helpless in real situations. The adepts said that these people had never even dreamed of the realms of experience that lay behind the phrases and texts they toyed with or worshiped.

For people who sought classic Zen authorities, the genuine teachers brought out anew the lesser known, more discursive teachings of the earlier great Zen masters, their lectures and letters. Case-books were put together showing contemporary teaching situations, with the more detailed comments of recent masters on psychological patterns and problems of the time. Contemporary letters and records of public talks by genuine teachers were gathered, printed, and circulated.

By such means the Zen masters of the thirteenth and fourteenth centuries worked to perpetuate their tradition of wisdom, which had become so overgrown with trailing vines of opinion, theory, sophistry and word-play. They knew that Zen sayings were not mere puzzles meant to amuse or befuddle or tickle the intellectual fancy. They continued to put Zen sayings to use as tools to help refine mind: to shift ordinary habits and errors of perception, to push people beyond piety and hopes of gain, to chart levels of progress, to illustrate moments of teaching, to map out reality. Such delicate instruments could only operate according to design in capable hands.

Many of the Zen masters of the Yuan period turned to a more direct discourse using blunt colloquial language and readily accessible metaphors. There is ample precedent for this down-home approach among the early masters of Zen, and colloquial language was normal in Zen literature. But in the Mongol period a more colloquial language emerged in many branches of culture. In the Yuan period as throughout the history of Zen, the most far-reaching principles of Buddhism were put across in colorful, basic language that made their personal implications hard to evade.

As the fourteenth century wore on, lip-service Zen proliferated, with its fancy, incomprehensible concoctions. Adepts complained that real Zen was being supplanted by false imitations, that the Zen gardens were becoming over-grown with weeds. Imitation Zen teachers multiplied, advertising their claims to membership in ancient mystic lineages. More and more the real teachers tended toward plainer language and back-to-basics reminders in their public lessons. They did not focus on their lineage credentials; for them the only criterion was real attainment, as defined by the Buddhist teachers of all times: independent knowledge, "teacherless wisdom," the direct experience of reality witnessed by the buddhas, the return to the source.

T'AEGO'S LIFE

T'aego was an outstanding Zen teacher in fourteenth-century Koryo, the National Teacher, the man from whom all the later lineages of Korean Zen claim ultimate descent. He was born in 1301 and died in 1382, after decades at work to further the Dharma. As a famous religious leader, he lived through the turbulent period when the cosmopolitan but oppressive Mongol rule over East Asia was broken, and new regimes were emerging over decades of struggle. His was the age when gunpowder weapons and firearms spread across the old world.

Early on T'aego committeed himself to the Buddhist life, and over the years he lived to the full many of its characteristic roles: youthful seeker, practicing discipline and traveling to Buddhist centers to seek wisdom; dedicated mystic, approaching wisdom with the cool intensity of the practical path; mature teacher, staying a while here and there to guide people and aid their development. In his fifties T'aego became a national figure: he was invited to the capital, pursued by high society and a fickle king, honored and exiled and honored again.

T'aego's "biography" is as frustrating as many other Zen biographies, which in general only mention key moments in a master's early life, relating incidents that epitomize his quest for enlightenment, without filling in all the details. The enlightenment stories only record the climax of a long process of effort. The main focus of Zen biographies is usually on a master's activities after enlightenment, after he appears in the world as a teacher. But here too only a few anecdotes may be recorded to stand for decades of a teaching career. Sometimes, as in T'aego's case, there are collections of recorded sayings that give a deeper view of a master's teaching style. But even then, if we compare what is recorded with all that the teacher said and did, it is like a handful of leaves out of all the leaves in the forest.

Reading these bare brief accounts of the religious feats of Zen masters, one might be tempted to imagine that these people never had any weaknesses to start with, that enlightenment came easy to them. But this would be a misreading of the stories. Zen biographies rarely dwell on the human frailties of Zen masters because this aspect was taken for granted. The significant part of the story for the Zen school was how the adepts rose above the basic limitations of ignorance, craving, and aggression, and what they accomplished afterward. A classic saying warns against the false image of the superhuman Zen master: "Everyone knows the achievement that crowns the age, but no one sees the sweating horses of antiquity."

T'aego's biography says little about his early life, except in a Buddhist context. He was born in 1301 in Kwangju, in the southern part of Korea. At thirteen, he was ordained a monk and began his studies. In his later teens and twenties he traveled around Korea visiting various temples and retreats to seek out teachers. Through his twenties T'aego meditated on the Zen case: "The myriad things return to one: what does the one return to?" He pursued this meditation until at thirty-two he was enlightened. Five years later came his decisive great enlightenment as he contemplated the Zen meditation-saying "[Does a dog have buddha-nature?] No."

As usual, we have a sparse list of key points, not a life story in the secular sense. T'aego may well have been from a devout Buddhist family, to be ordained so young, or perhaps he was a boy with an early religious bent. Traveling in search of teachers was the normal course for a young Zen monk: hoping to meet a flesh-and-blood representative of the Dharma who could show him a living road. (Social restraints on women traveling made it harder for them in the Zen Path.) The custom of traveling to various Zen centers was a way to institutionalize the idea that formalism and rote learning were not enough, that real work under a real expert was necessary.

T'aego's enlightenment story centers on his meditation work with two Zen sayings, but from his writings we can be sure that he had made a deep study of the Buddhist scriptures, Buddhist philosophy, and Zen lore as a whole. The details of how he found the Path and exactly how he practiced in his early years were not recorded as such: the record just says that he meditated on Zen sayings.

This method was in use in the Zen school over the centuries, and many famous teachers spoke on how to do it. T'aego's own lessons on the subject are translated below (items 12 to 16). In this method, the person directs his or her attention onto a Zen saying used as the meditation point, and, with persistence, learns to keep it there with more and more consistency and continuity. Gradually the mind of the practitioner fuses with the meditation point and opens up to its message. The Zen sayings are meant as compact codes that open up a window on enlightened perception.

The meditation points used here are the public cases of Zen, which may be short sayings, philosophical propositions, or interaction scenes and dialogues. As the person keeps in contact with the case, the layers of meaning within it are designed to interact with the person's conceptual mind and habitual frame of reference, to loosen their grip on the mind and to let the person experience a wider reality. Gradually concepts and motivational patterns are rearranged, until one day suddenly the person begins to see as the buddhas see. According to the traditional account, and judging by the evidence of the writings of the adepts themselves, this happened to T'aego and to countless others in the Zen school.

How would we know how the buddhas see? The Zen school answers: because they told us in the scriptures, and the Zen classics tell us too. A person meditating who sensed some progress or insight could turn to these for confirmation. These teachings were highly venerated as a repository of the enlightened insights of illustrious predecessors, a map and a guide for learners.

Three years after his great enlightenment, at the age of forty, T'aego came to Chunghung Temple on Three Corners Mountain in Hanyang (modern Seoul) and began to teach. Students of Buddhism flocked to him there, and he became a well-known teacher.

In 1346 T'aego set out for China. He came to the great capital of the Yuan empire (modern Beijing). In 1347 he headed for South China to call on Zen masters there.

T'aego had intended to visit the noted teacher Zhuyuan, but since he died before T'aego arrived, T'aego went to see another eminent Zen expert, Shiwu. When T'aego showed him his writings, Shiwu was greatly impressed and questioned him closely. (The medium of communication was probably written Chinese.)

Shiwu said, "Since you have already passed through this realm, do you know that there is also the barrier of the ancestral teachers?" T'aego said, "What barrier is there?"

Shiwu said,"With what you have attained, your meditation work is correct and your perception is clear. Nevertheless, you should abandon every single bit of it. Otherwise, it will become obstruction-by-truth and block correct perception." T'aego said, "I abandoned it long ago." Shiwu said, "Then let's stop for now."

The next day T'aego went before Shiwu with full formality of deportment.

Shiwu said, "Buddha to buddha, enlightened teacher to enlightened teacher, they have only transmitted Mind: there is no other dharma."

"As soon as there is a bit of illumination, if you think it is real, you fall into the reflections of the light, and plan to make your living there."

"Having seen that this is a human defect which people are helpless to deal with, in order to restrain it, all the enlightened teachers since antiquity have therefore set up a barrier in the realm of pure evenness. If you really penetrate through it, then it's all an obsolete device."

Here Shiwu is pointing to the danger of the "fall at the peak," the infatuation with the pure truth aspect of reality, settling down in its peace and bliss and quietude, rather than returning to the world as a bodhisattva. From the point of view of the seeker, the "realm of pure evenness" seems like a supreme achievement; to the adept already there, it is a barrier that must be passed through. Complete enlightenment in Buddhism means that neither pure nor impure realms present obstructions or provoke attachments.

Shiwu continued, "But in a land with no people [to guide you], how did you discern the fork in the road so clearly?"

T'aego replied, "Because it is all there in the expedient teachings imparted by the buddhas and enlightened ancestors."

Shiwu said, "Very good! If you had not planted a correct basis for enlightenment in previous births, you too would have been ensnared in the net of falsity.

"Though I live here on a remote mountain, I am always setting forth the gate of the Zen ancestors. I have been waiting for a descendant like you for a long time."

T'aego replied, "An enlightened good friend like you is hard to encounter even over endless ages. I vow not to leave your side."

Shiwu told him, "I too want to savor this quiet solitude together with you, but I'm afraid [if we stayed together too long] later on there would be no way for you to leave, and this would be detrimental to the Dharma. Better stay and talk for half a month, and then go back."

Bodhisattvas do not indulge their own enjoyment of the fruits of liberation, but have a duty to the Dharma: they must return among the unenlightened to spread the teaching of enlightenment, and thereby "repay the benevolence" of the enlightened ones who showed them the way.

The meeting between T'aego and Shiwu is the most detailed episode in his biography, because to the Zen school their encounter was laden with deep significance.

The bonds of mutual respect between Shiwu and T'aego as companions in the Dharma can best be seen in the letters between them translated below (items 128 to 130).

Shiwu regarded T'aego, some thirty years his junior, as an independently enlightened man, qualified by his own direct experience to represent the Dharma—the kind of worthy successor a teacher waits for. T'aego looked up to Shiwu as the consummate master who set the final seal on his enlightenment, an enlightened elder with the full intimate knowledge of the Path necessary to certify his own arrival. Shiwu as the senior man reminded T'aego of his duty to uphold the Dharma for its own sake, without compromising with worldly sentiments, and thus to continue the tradition of the Zen ancestors.

After leaving Shiwu, T'aego returned to North China to the Yuan capital, where he was invited to Eternal Peace Zen Temple by the emperor and given a golden robe as a mark of honor. T'aego's talks there (items 1 to 7) were attended by the Mongol high nobility, whom he humbly saluted and then sharply reminded of their obligations to society and to Buddhism.

T'aego returned to Korea in 1348. He went back to Mount Sosol in his home area, and for four years lived by farming.

By the 1350's the Yuan dynasty was tottering, deeply shaken by the millenarian revolts across central China. The Koryo king Kongmin, who came to the throne in 1352, took the opportunity to try to reassert Korean independence from the Mongols. For King Kongmin, this meant a long piecemeal process of trying to overthrow or co-opt the entrenched grandees and military nobles who ruled the country under Mongol domination. Many of these aristocrats had their own forces and bases and recognized legitimacy as regional lords. While the upheaval in China ultimately broke the Yuan power there, it did not settle the conflicts in Korea between pro- and anti-Mongol aristocrats and their parties.

The political struggle in Korea was not only a matter of rivalries among the landed aristocracy and local strongmen and Mongol garrisons. With the fragmentation of power, coastal Korea (like coastal China and Japan) became vulnerable to the large-scale raids of pirate bands operating from the offshore island. As in the contemporary Western world, commerce and piracy were on continuum. Given the state's proclivity to monopolize trade, independent seafarers were often condemned as smugglers and pirates anyway. Already organized in secret and armed for self-protection, they could emerge on the offensive whenever the central power waned, to strike wherever disorganized defenses made it easy and profitable. In 1351 even the Koryo capital was hit by marauders.

Throughout the agricultural countryside, the open struggle among local powerholders undermined the integrity of the whole system of control. There was the added strain caused by contending claimants on land revenue and labor power, and the spectacle of local rulers being ousted and replaced. Under pressure to maintain their power-bases, the local strongmen often found they needed to conciliate the people beneath them, to ensure social peace and keep food and crafts production going. There were serf and slave outbreaks: chasing off overseers, abolishing dues, burning the documents that defined their hereditary servitude. Usually these were quite localized, and would be put down when the upper class regrouped and managed to field a superior military force. But in the two generations of unrest from about 1350 to the establishment of the new regime around 1390, resistance from below generally won concessions.

People of rank and property were terrified by the large-scale invasions of millenarian armies in 1359 and 1362. The military men who became the great hegemons of the next generation and "reestablished order" originally came on the scene as local commanders who drove back the tide of rebellion and anarchy-from-below. Of course it took them thirty years more to quell persistent anarchy-from-above.

King Kongmin began his efforts to reestablish the Koryo dynasty's power on coming to the throne in 1352. Not only did he face the remaining Mongol bases in Koryo; the king met with bitter opposition among the established grandees when he ennobled his own followers and through them tried to centralize power in his own hands. He abolished the state council that represented the political interests of the grandees under the Mongol rulers. The king survived being formally deposed by the Yuan dynasty, and many direct attempts by aristocratic enemies to strike him down. There were many twists and turns over two decades. The Mongols suffered key reverses, but other rival powers within Korea persisted and even grew in strength, and King Kongmin did not live to see his own unchallenged supremacy. Aristocratic assassins struck Kongmin down in 1374, and a pro-Mongol king was put on the throne. The man who was to be the founder of the next dynasty, Yi Song-gye, was already an influential regional military commander in the northeast, still a dozen years from supreme power.

T'aego was summoned to the capital in 1352 when Kongmin assumed the throne. The story goes that T'aego lectured the king on the need to clean up the government and remove evildoers from power. The king responded that Mongol pressures limited what he could do. T'aego told the king that no matter how great his zeal for Buddhism, if he proved unable to manage national affairs, there would be no merit. He advised Kongmin not to build any new Buddhist temples, but to content himself with repairing the ones founded by the first king of the Koryo dynasty. T'aego also repeated the traditional warnings against sacrificing agricultural land to the needs of the military.

T'aego's reputation preceded him, and when he came to the capital he was besieged by would-be seekers of all ranks. Evidently T'aego judged that conditions were not right for more public teaching: having done what he could for the time being, he returned to rustic Mount Sosol.

Another royal invitation came in 1356. T'aego was brought into the Inner Buddha Hall in the palace and invested with official regalia in front of a large assembly of the nobility and many leading monks. He was designated Royal Teacher. For two years T'aego acted as the arbiter of the Buddhist establishment, passing judgment on those who sought royal sanction for their religious claims, naming abbots at the major temples.

T'aego used his power to try to overcome the sectarian differences that had grown within Koryo Zen. This is how he explained the situation:

> These days each of the Nine Mountains Zen sects takes pride in its own way of thinking and thinks that the others are inferior, while its own is the best. The arguments and conflicts grow ever more serious, and recently they have even taken up arms and built fortifications for their sectarian interests.
>
> Thus they injure the harmony of the Buddhist community and destroy correct norms. Alas! Zen is one single school, but people fight among themselves and make it into many sects. They do not abide in the everywhere-equal selfless Path of their own fundamental teachers, the style of purity and rest, outside of conventions, the style of the line of Zen teachers. Nor do they abide by the intent of the First Kings when they protected the truth and put the nation at peace.

T'aego therefore advocated a reunification of the Zen establishment, and renewal of the original intent. As a standard for a reformed Zen community, he proposed the well-known *Pure Rules of Baizhang,* a ninth-century classic by one of the great Zen masters, widely in print in the thirteenth and fourteenth centuries. Among other things, Baizhang prescribed practical self-supporting labor for Zen monks.

In 1356 King Kongmin scored a major military victory over the Mongols and began to move to dismantle their network of vassals. This provoked intense resistance, and the capital was gripped by tension and intrigue among the high nobility.

In 1357 T'aego asked to be allowed to go home, but permission was refused. T'aego left the capital anyway by stealth. After a while King Kongmin relented, granted T'aego formal permission to retire, and sent along his emblems of rank.

In 1362 T'aego was again summoned by the king, and ordered to teach at Phoenix Cliff Zen Temple on Mount Huiyang and then at Precious Forest Zen Temple on Mount Kaji. After four years' service, T'aego returned emblems of rank and begged to be allowed to depart. This time King Kongmin acceded to his request and let him withdraw. It was 1366: T'aego was sixty-five years old.

1366 marked the beginning of the ascendancy of the upstart monk Sinton, who became Kongmin's favorite. The king heaped honors and titles on the low-born Sinton, who became the chief executor of a new push for political reforms aimed at cutting back the power of the aristocracy and strengthening the royal government. Sinton used his influence with the king to amass riches for himself and lived in extravagant luxury. He encompassed the downfall of many of Kongmin's aristocratic enemies, and naturally became the target of bitter resentment and slander.

T'aego traveled to South China in 1368. Perhaps he left Korea to avoid the schemes of Sinton, who resented

T'aego as a threat to his own religious pretensions. Perhaps he wanted to renew contacts with the Zen communities in China, and assess the new situation there. There was much to see, much change since his visit twenty years before. After two decades of warfare, relative stability had been restored: 1368 was the year the Ming dynasty was proclaimed. In his own way the new Chinese emperor believed in Buddhism, and indeed sponsored giant public ceremonies and conclaves of leading monks. But the Ming emperor also decreed a system of laws meant to control Buddhism tightly, to limit the freedom of monks and nuns to move among the people, and above all to stamp out millenarian tendencies. Unfortunately there is no record of the real nature of T'aego's activities on this visit to China.

Back in the Korean capital Sinton spread the story that T'aego had gone abroad to plot sedition, and persuaded King Kongmin to strip T'aego of his rank and honors and have him defrocked. But the next year the king changed his mind, pardoned T'aego, and allowed him to return to Korea, to Mount Sosol in his home district.

With the demise of Sinton in 1371, T'aego was restored to the rank of National Teacher. Despite his attempts to decline, he was appointed abbot of Shining Source Temple, and spent seven years there. In 1381 he moved to Yangsan-sa; when the new king visited the temple, T'aego, now eighty, was again given the title of National Teacher. In 1382 T'aego returned to Mount Sosol, where he died. The court bestowed on him the posthumous epithet "Zen Master of Perfect Realization."

Like the rest of T'aego's biography, the account of his later decades is no more than a bare outline. Much of what T'aego did as a Buddhist teacher naturally took place in intimate face-to-face interactions, and was not recorded for posterity. All that is left for us to study is the brief record of some of his writings and public talks, translated below.

T'aego's role as a public figure in Korean history is harder to judge from this distance, with only tendentious accounts to rely on. What was T'aego trying to accomplish in politics? Can we today know enough of the day-to-day inner life of the fourteenth-century Koryo elite even to imagine the real options available to a Zen teacher trying to influence them?

As substitute for a detailed, informed view of the contemporary possibilities, it is easier to judge history in terms of modern preoccupations: whose side are you on in medieval history? The view of T'aego then becomes a function of the verdict on King Kongmin. Was Kongmin a nationalist, an ally of progressive forces (the local gentry against the Mongol-connected grandees)? Or was the king a superstitious, self-aggrandizing tyrant, inconsistent, decadent, the tool of his favorites, a political failure? Was Sinton a true monk-of-the-people, stepping forward to assist his king in progressive reforms? Or was he a vile upstart, a vicious political schemer? Even if such questions could be impartially decided, would this necessarily locate T'aego or show how the contemporary world appeared to a Zen master?

What was T'aego doing when he preached to the high and mighty and accepted honors and positions from them? He gives us his own answer in his talk on "Making the Nation Great" (item 7).

Evidently he had no love of rank and honor and golden robes for their own sakes, or he would not have waited so long to take advantage of his fame to get them, or repeatedly withdrawn from the capital once high position was within reach. If he had been currying favor, he would not have addressed the Mongol and Korean nobility with such blunt, uncompromising admonitions, or criticized the Buddhist establishment so pointedly for going to ruin. Then again, if he had been seeking a peaceful life as a religious recluse (wrongly imagined to be the goal of Buddhism), he would never have become involved with high society in the capital, which was an extremely dangerous environment, poisoned by ambition, factionalism, and revenge.

If we accept his credentials as a Buddhist teacher, T'aego must have seen some opportunities to advance the Dharma by taking on such a public role. In his public talks to the people in power, T'aego stressed traditional Confucian and Buddhist themes, peppered with the challenging direct tone of a Zen master. He urged them to follow the example of the legendary ancient Sage Emperors Yao and Shun, whose rule was welcomed by the people because it was fairminded and realistically concerned with their welfare. T'aego reminded the high and mighty that they could not escape the consequences of their acts. He urged them to live up to their duty as protectors of the Dharma. He told them that to be genuine patrons of Buddhism, secular lords had to be like father and mother to the common people.

T'aego knew he could not remake King Kongmin or the courtiers whom he lectured. But perhaps he found it possible now and then to push them in the right direction. He could not reform the Zen community at one stroke, but he could use his power in the Dharma and his temporal power under the king to try to redirect the Korean Zen world away from sectarian quarrels.

Expressing what modern people would call political commitment, T'aego said this:

> Among the common people, there are indeed those loyal to the lord and filial to their parents, those who possess talent and virtue. Though they may be abandoned among the weeds they still have concerns for the trend of the times, and are intent on saving the world and its people. Though I am stupid and unworthy, because I could not bear to be silent in the face of so many concerns, I have been introduced in the highest circles.
>
> If those in power rewarded the worthy and good

and punished the wicked and the deceitful, who would not be loyal? Who would not be filial? Who would be without the Path, without moral orientation? Who wouldn't study? Who wouldn't cultivate his own virtue?

Nevertheless, if there is anyone here with the strength to uproot mountains and the energy to top the world, let him come forward and fight alongside me. Let us sacrifice our bodies for the nation, and accomplish the great enterprise. This is not only for the great nobles. If there are no such people here among you, then the old monk T'aego goes off to serve in the border forts by himself with a single horse and spear.

T'aego's own words are the only indisputable evidence of his Buddhist mission. They are respectfully translated here to give the modern reader a chance to get acquainted with this buddha from Korea.

Collected Sayings of T'aego

According to the preface, T'aego's teaching words were collected by Kim Chung-hyon around 1356, and this record was followed by Chong Mong-ju, the writer of this collection, in 1388.

1. PUBLIC AND PRIVATE

When T'aego occupied the abbot's seat at Yongning Temple (in Beijing), he brandished his staff and said: "Here is the great furnace and bellows for melting down buddhas and patriarchs, the hammer and tongs for forging birth and death. Those who confront its point lose their courage. Don't be surprised that I have no face."

He brandished the staff again and said: "All the hundreds of thousands of buddhas disintegrate right here."

Again he brandished the staff; then he held it up and said: "This is it. When the whale drinks the ocean dry, it reveals the coral branches."

T'aego held up the robe [emblematic] of succession and said: "This piece of cowhide is the symbol that the bloodline of the buddhas and patriarchs has not been broken off. Old Shakyamuni could not use it up in thirty-nine years [of teaching] at more than three hundred assemblies. At the end, at the assembly on Spirit Peak, he entrusted it to [Kashyapa], the golden-hued ascetic, and said: 'Pass it on from generation to generation, until the last age, and do not let it be cut off.' Obviously, obviously."

T'aego held up the golden Dharma-robe and said: "Why has this golden monk's robe come from the lord's palace today? Haven't you read [in the *Benevolent King Sutra*] that this Dharma has been entrusted to the monarch and the great ministers?"

He held up the robe [emblematic] of the succession and said: "This one is a private matter intimately transmitted from father to son."

He held up the golden robe and said: "This one is a public matter bestowed by the royal house. The private is not equal to the public: the public comes before the private."

Then he put on the golden robe, lifted up one corner of it, and called to the assembly: "Do you see this one? Not only am I glad to receive it and wear it humbly, but it has already wrapped up numberless buddhas and patriarchs."

T'aego gave a shout and held up the robe [emblematic] of succession and said: "Does everyone clearly witness this? This is something evil transmitted from [my teacher to me on] Mount Xiawu."

Then he put it on, pointed to the teacher's seat, and said: "The one road on top of Vairocana's head is very clear. Does everyone see where the road begins?"

Then T'aego climbed the stairs saying, "One, two, three, four, five."

He ascended to the teacher's seat carrying incense and said: "This incense has no coming or going; it mysteriously pervades past, present, and future. It is not inside or outside; it penetrates all directions. I salute the august personage of the present emperor of the great Yuan dynasty, the lord of the world. May he live for ten thousand years, for ten thousand times ten thousand years. I humbly hope that his golden orb will enjoy sovereignty over the three thousand worlds, that his jade leaves will be fragrant for a million million springs."

Then T'aego held up the incense and said: "This incense is clean and pure. It contains myriad virtues. It is serene and at ease, and secures thousands of blessing. I respectfully wish that all the queen mother's family will preserve their good health and tranquillity, and live as long as heaven. May the glory of this dragon's progeny know an eternal spring, and never grow old, enjoying the happiness of being the mother of the monarch."

Then he lifted the incense and said: "As I hold up this incense, heaven is high and earth deep. If I put it down, the ocean is deep and the rivers are pure. I respectfully wish that the crown prince may live a thousand years, a thousand years, and another thousand years. May he traverse jade realms for a thousand years of happiness and serve the Heavenly Visage [of the emperor] with filial piety for ten thousand years of joy."

Then T'aego held up a stick of incense he had inside his robe and said: "The buddhas and patriarchs do not know this incense, and ghosts and spirits cannot fathom it. It was not born of heaven and earth, nor was it gained spontaneously. In the past, while traveling on foot in Korea, I came to a patron's garden, and under a shadowless tree, I encountered this thing with no edges or seams or place to get a grip. I came to a ten-thousand-fathom cliff, and let go with my whole body. There was no breath of life at all, when suddenly I came to life again, floating at ease. Nevertheless, people doubted me, and I thought there would be no one to give clear proof. The more I hid it, the stronger it became; the more I wanted to hide it, the more it was evident. My evil repute and stinking smell filled the world, and today I obey the imperial command [to become abbot here], and hold it up before you.

"In front of this assembly of gods and humans, I burn [this incense] in the brazier. I offer it up to [my former teacher], Master Shiwu, who formerly dwelled at Fuyuan Puhui Zen Temple in West Zhe circuit, and who has retired to a hut on the peak of Mount Xiawu. I offer it to him to repay his kindness in attesting [to my enlightenment]."

2. OVER THE PEAK WITH COLORED CLOUDS

When T'aego sat in the teacher's seat, the elder Zhantang of Xinghua Baoen Zen Temple struck the gavel and announced: "O dragons and elephants attending this Dharma assembly, you must contemplate the supreme truth. The teacher will now reveal the guiding principle."

T'aego brandished his staff and said: "This staff and the sound of the gavel have already clearly explained the supreme truth for you. Is there anyone here who recognizes the benevolence and can repay it? Come forward and give us proof."

At the time there was a monk who asked: "With etiquette, each person has a defined status. Without etiquette, relations between teacher and pupil lack decorum. Which is right?"

T'aego said: "Why must you get up only to fall down?"

The monk continued: "Today by imperial command you open this teaching hall, and ascend the jewel seat. Gods and humans have gathered from all over: host and guests have come together. I wonder, Teacher, whose family song do you sing? Whose family style do you inherit?"

T'aego said: "Over the peak with colored clouds, the moon of a thousand ages comes to shine on the palace of great illumination."

The questioner continued: "Then after Shakyamuni and before Maitreya, the treasury of the eye of the correct teaching, the wondrous mind of nirvana, is initially in your hands. Let go, and all the buddhas and bodhisattvas are congratulating you. Hold fast, and even the Zen patriarchs have no way to look up to you. I wonder whether today you will let go or hold fast?"

T'aego said: "All the stars in the sky salute the north, all the streams on earth flow east."

The monk went on: "If so, then ultimately the streams

must flow into the sea, and the clouds must seek the mountains to return to."

T'aego said: "You are a fine lion cub, but you're still yapping like a wild fox."

The monk continued: "Sometimes the tathagata takes on the body of Indra, sometimes the body of a king. What buddhas is the present monarch an incarnation of?"

T'aego said: "The Primordial Buddha."

The questioner went on: "This is the second phrase. What is the first phrase?"

T'aego then gave a shout.

The monk continued: "In the past at the assembly on Spirit Peak, today in the hall of Yongning: is it the same or different?"

T'aego said: "See for yourself: is it the same or different?"

The monk continued: "The present august monarch, beyond his myriad concerns of state, has set his mind on Zen and promoted the correct Dharma, so that the Buddhist institutions have someone to rely on. I wonder what dharma you will use to repay the imperial benevolence?"

T'aego said: "I pick up it up sideways and use it upside down without a set pattern. I wish our monarch above a million million springs."

The monk continued: "The patrons of this temple, the grandees and high officials [gathered here] honor the Dharma gate, and have created this excellent situation. What lucky omen will we have?"

T'aego said: "Unicorns and phoenixes present lucky omens. Tortoises and dragons conquer the great capital."

3. STOP ASKING

There was another monk [who wanted to ask questions], but as soon as he came forward, T'aego held him back with his whisk and said: "Stop asking. Even if countless millions and billions of buddhas came forth all at once, each with unobstructed ability to preach, uttering infinite oceans of words, with each word imbued with endless eloquence, and posed thousands of questions, clouds of questions, it would not take a single grunt of mine to answer them all totally. Even if such questions and such answers go on all the time without interruption until Maitreya comes down to be born [on earth] these are just the doings of karmic consciousness, with no connection to the fundamental matter. Even more useless are stitched-together phrases and rhetorical barbs: not only do they bury the vehicle of the supreme school, but they lose you the nostrils your momma bore you with.

"This is why, since antiquity, the buddhas and patriarchs have not established texts or words [as sacred. Rather,] they have transmitted mind with mind and sealed truth with truth, taking it up generation after generation, passing it on without end. Even today, the right people for it are not lacking.

"Let's leave this aside for now. What is the vehicle of the school of transcendence?"

After a long silence, T'aego said: "If I brought this up, I'm afraid there would be no one to accept it. Even so, when we get to this stage, no name can be used, not 'buddha,' not 'patriarch,' not 'patchrobed monk,' not 'four fruits' or 'the three sagely paths' or 'the ten stages,' not 'inherent enlightenment' or 'wondrous enlightenment,' not 'nirvana' or 'birth and death,' not 'the eighty-four thousand perfections' or 'the eighty-four thousand afflictions.' The whole great canon of verbal teachings is idle words, the seventeen hundred Zen stories are sleep talk. Linji's shouts and Deshan's blows are child's play.

"Haven't you read the ancient's saying? 'With the gate shut, sleeping, we receive those of the highest potential. Looking on solicitously, we bend for those of middle and lower potentials. How could we be in the teacher's seat and sport demon eyes?' This is a commonplace saying, but still rather effective.

"When I teach like this, it is like the white sun in the blue sky, like speaking of dreams without dreaming, like cutting a wound in flesh. When you check it out, I deserve a blow of the staff. Isn't there anyone here now with a poison hand? If there is, he can repay the benevolence that cannot be repaid, and assist in the uncontrived teaching. If not, I carry out this imperative anyway."

Suddenly T'aego took the staff and brandished it once saying: "The whole world is at peace."

He brandished the staff again and said: "The Buddha-sun flourishes again."

He shook the staff twice in succession and gave a shout.

4. A ZEN STORY

T'aego cited [this Zen case]: "When Baoshou opened his teaching hall, Sansheng pushed forward a monk, whom Baoshou immediately hit. Sansheng said, 'If this is the way you help people, you are blinding the eyes of everyone in this city.' Baoshou then returned to his abbot's room."

T'aego commented: "These two old awls! One is like the dragon king from the bottom of the ocean, making Sumeru shake so he can seize the giant bird's eggs. One is like the giant garuda-bird king, parting the ocean so he can seize the dragon's children. Both men display their supernatural powers to the full. Both are equipped with devices to kill and to give life, and the manners of both guest and host. Punches and kicks come one after another, singing and clapping respond to each other. At the crossroads they calculate their food money and distribute it to everyone, without leaving anything out. They may be good, they may be wondrous, but when we check them out, there's still this one.

"Baoshou opened the teaching hall—the embryo of disaster is born. Sansheng pushed forward a monk—adding frost to snow. Baoshou immediately hit him—as always, playing with the spirit. Sansheng said, 'If this is the way you help people, you are blinding the eyes of everyone in the city'—he doesn't recognize his own mistake. Baoshou returned to the abbot's room—a tiger with a scorched tail.

"But tell me, have I ever been checked out by anyone or not? Listen to a verse:

> I rent a room by the south wall of the city
> Contentedly I lie drunk at home
> Suddenly I hear the emperor's decree
> After saluting, I head for what's left in the wine jar
> Freezing cold in my bones
> Windblown snow beating against my windows
> Fire in the earthen stove in the middle of the night
> The tea is brewed, the fragrance wafts from the pot

T'aego tapped three times on the corner of the meditation bench with his whisk, struck the gavel, and said: "Observe carefully the Dharma of the Dharma King. The teaching of the king of the teaching is like this."

Then he left the teacher's seat.

5. A TALK TO THE MIGHTY

In 1347, on the sixth day of the third month, the emperor of the Great Yuan invited T'aego to Fengen, serving the Imperial Benevolence Zen Temple [within the Yongning complex]. After salutations to his majesty, T'aego went up to the teaching hall, pointed to the main temple gate, and said:

"The Great Path has no gate: where do all of you people intend to enter it? Bah! The universal gate of perfect penetration is wide open."

At the buddha shrine T'aego said: "Two thousand years ago, I was you. Two thousand years later, you are me. It has almost leaked out." Then he bowed three times.

At the shrine of the founder of the Koryo kingdom,

T'aego said: "You are the grand ancestor of Korea. I am the king of the myriad dharmas. In the old days we met and discussed this matter. Right now we meet again and discuss it in secret." Then he gave a shout.

In the abbot's room, T'aego said: "This is a den of idle spirits and wild demons. Suddenly today the sound of thunder shakes the earth: I wonder where it disperses to?" He brandished his staff once and said: "When the people scatter from the sandbar, the seagulls become the lords."

Occupying the room, T'aego brandished his staff and said: "Here, if buddhas come, I will hit them; if patriarchs come, I will hit them." Again he brandished the staff.

The state councillor Li Qixian handed the imperial rescript [naming him abbot there] to T'aego. T'aego took it and showed it to the assembly and said: "Does anyone know whether or not the monarch, who protects the True Dharma, who protects the nation and the people, has entered into the samadhi of the techniques of the enlightened teachers? If you cannot see, I'll trouble the duty distributor to display this to the assembly."

After the duty distributor had shown the imperial rescript to everyone, T'aego picked up the embroidered monk's robe [bestowed on him by the emperor] and said:

"This embroidered monk's robe was tailored by our benevolent monarch in all sincerity, wielding the cutting edge of wisdom. It was made with utmost dedication. Five-colored clouds stretch across it; it sparkles with the lights of stars from the heaven of righteousness. It is circled about with the seven gems; the waves on the ocean of wisdom are vast and pure. Rose-colored vapors waft up from the red city. Fragrant smoke with the luster of jade rises in lush peaks. Wonderfully rare birds and beasts offer up auspicious omens of ten thousand generations of splendor for our lord. Propitious grasses and flowers open up everlasting years of springtime beauty for our lady.

"It is not Locana's precious imperial vestment. It is not

Shakyamuni's tattered robe. But tell me, who is qualified to put it on?" . . .

T'aego held up the robe [emblematic] of the Dharma and said: "This monk's robe covered with embroidery has been passed on by the buddhas and patriarchs since antiquity. It is an unexcelled field of blessings, a garment of great liberation. Our great teacher Shakyamuni handed it on to Mahakashyapa, and it was passed down through the generations to the thirty-third patriarch, the venerable Huineng, the 'Great Mirror.' Then, because of the dissension [surrounding its transmission, the practice of passing on the emblematic robe] was stopped [by Huineng].

"So why is it brought forth today from the royal palace and given into my hands? The prairie fire does not burn up everything: when the spring wind blows, life is born again."

T'aego then called to the assembly, saying: "All of you should put it on along with me!" T'aego and the whole crowd [made the gesture] of putting it on together at the same time. Then T'aego lifted up one corner [of the robe] and called to the assembly: "Do you see? Not only have all of you put it on along with me, but everything everywhere in all the worlds in the ten directions—the sky and the earth, the dense array of myriad forms, the saintly and the ordinary, the sentient and the insentient—have all put it on at once. Bah!"

T'aego pointed to the teacher's seat and said: "Hundreds and thousands of buddhas and patriarchs have farted here, filling the whole world with the stench. Today I have no choice but to pour the waters of the four oceans over it and make it clean. Don't everyone say that this is even more embarrassing."

T'aego ascended to the seat, and held up incense, saying: "This incense is rooted in the countless worlds of the universe and its leaves cover millions of polar mountains. We offer it up to salute the Great Yuan Son of Heaven, our present august emperor. May he live ten thousand

years, ten thousand thousand years! I humbly hope that
this virtue may reach ten thousand lands, forever resplendent with the radiance of [the sage emperor] Shun, which
is Great Peace. May his benevolence shower down on the
whole world, forever fanning the wind of [the sage em-
peror] Yao, which is Non-doing."

After dedicating incense to the members of the royal
family and high nobles assembled there, T'aego continued: "I humbly hope that birth after birth you will continue forever as the loyal ministers of the emperor, secur-
ing the Kingly Way within [the state], and that lifetime
after lifetime you will always be good friends to the buddhas and patriarchs, protecting the Dharma gate outside
[in society]. This incense has been passed on from buddha
to buddha, transmitted from enlightened teacher to enlightened teacher. When it meets with respect, it is more
valuable than the whole world. When it meets with scorn,
it is not worth a cent.

"Now it is the *ding-hai* year of the reign-period Zhi
Zheng, 'Perfection of Orthodoxy' [1347]. The Great Yuan
rule all under heaven. Here in the teaching hall at Yongning Temple, I obey the imperial rescript, and propagate
the Dharma in this deceptive way, in order to enable humans and devas to witness it together, to suddenly leap to
the land of the Buddha of Unmoving Wisdom.

"Time and circumstances were not right, so I went to
Sosol Mountain and passed the days with the streams and
rocks, savoring together the solitude and silence, to wait
out my remaining years. Now suddenly I must obey the
command of another invitation from His Majesty, who is
not unmindful of our former pact [for me to be at his
service]. Here inside Fengen Temple, at Sumeru Platform,
in front of an assembly of humans and devas, for those
who have not yet seen or heard of [the Dharma], I bring
it out anew."

As the incense was set alight in the burner, T'aego said:
"This is offered to the great Zen teacher of the South,

Master Shiwu. I use it to repay the benevolence of the Dharma-milk [he fed me].

"If you affirm [relative reality], you are calling gold yellow. If you deny [its existence], the unicorn has one horn [absolute subsumes relative, God is one]. Go ahead and discuss and assess it wrongly."

6. THE SUPREME TRUTH

As T'aego went to the teacher's seat, the head monk of the temple struck the gavel and announced: "O great assembly of dragons and elephants to the Dharma meeting! Observe the supreme truth!"

To bring up the general guiding principles, T'aego said: "The one road of transcendence is not transmitted by the thousand sages. But tell me, what is it that's not transmitted? Here, if you get entangled the least little bit, you go wrong by ten thousand miles. Those who know now to ask are given thirty blows, and those who don't know how to ask are given thirty blows."

[Some questions and answers went unrecorded.] T'aego then said:

"Old Shakyamuni said, 'The enlightenment of all the buddhas is far beyond all words and talk.' So how could the work in our supreme school's vehicle use doings or words? Contrived doings are playing with the spirit. Words are the dregs. As for the true correct way of showing [reality], all the buddhas of past, present and future 'hang their mouths on the wall' and all the generations of enlightened teachers hide their bodies in the weeds. Linji shouted when they entered the gate; Deshan hit them: what child's play!

"Knowing early on that it is like this, I was forced to take my empty hands and wander like a cloud over the world seeking teachers and inquiring after the Path. It was like putting a head on top of a head. It also attracted suspicion from people. Looking back on it coldly, it embarrasses me to death. In the past in my native land I hid myself in the mountain valleys and did not sell the Buddha Dharma cheap to worldly people, or bury the wind of Zen [in worldly concerns]. I have just gone on this way, totally at ease, expansive and free, independent, happy, alive.

"My whole life an empty reputation has lingered [around me]. Today I go too far by accepting another invitation from the king of the realm. I ascend to this seat, and look out on a sea of faces. I don't know what to do about you, I can only chatter on. All of you will think, 'Today an enlightened teacher appears in the world.' What a joke!

"When I talk like this, it's already sleep talk. Why are all of you sleeping with your eyes open?"

T'aego brandished his staff and said: "This happy assembly was convened by [our patrons], the Source of the Myriad Transformations, Mother of the Myriad Virtues, Whose Virtue Covers Countless Worlds, Whose Capacity Encompasses the Universe, Sage Among Sages, the Great Yuan Son of Heaven, and Worthy Among Worthies, the King of this land. Their benevolence flows on for ten thousand generations, with the Path as their deep concern. They are like the moonlight in the sky, with humane concern for their fellow men as their governing policy. The white sun is at high noon. At precisely this time, the incense billows up from the golden censer, slowly seeping into the jade palace. How can I, T'aego, a minor monk, salute them?"

He brandished his staff again and said: "When the Path [the Dao, the moral orientation of society and its members] is secure, the orders of the emperor do not need to be transmitted. When the era is one of purity, they stop extolling utopia."

[Later at the same session T'aego said:]

"In the old days the emperor Wu of the Liang dynasty received the enlightened teacher Bodhidharma with full ceremony. Then he asked: 'What is the highest meaning of the holy truths?' Bodhidharma said: "Empty, without holiness.' The emperor asked: 'Who is the one facing me now?' Bodhidharma said: 'I don't know.'

"This is the model of the first communication of the message of Zen in the eastern lands. Today the king of our country has invited me, a minor monk, to talk about the vehicle of the Zen school. I salute His Imperial Majesty, Her Imperial Majesty, the Imperial Crown Prince above, the great assembly of humans and devas in between, and the officials and commoners below, for bestowing the great gift of the Dharma. I have not said a word, and Their Majesties have not asked a word. Has it been the same as or different from the questions and answers between Emperor Wu and Bodhidharma? If you can tell, I'll allow you one eye. If you cannot tell, listen to a verse:

> The high ancient's voice is closest
> Too bad the season is spring when the blossoms fall
> I urge you to drain another cup of wine
> At the gate where the sun rises in the west,
>   there are no old acquaintances

7. MAKING THE NATION GREAT

On the fifteenth day of the first month of 1357 [in Kaesong, the Korean capital], T'aego went up to the teaching hall at the Temple for the Protection of the Military in the royal palace. After dedicating the incense, T'aego took the seat and held up the rescript [summoning him there] and said:

"The samadhis of the buddhas—the buddhas do not know them. Our present monarch protects and upholds the Buddha Dharma. The samadhis are all right here: who can truly master them?

"Let me trouble the duty distributor to read out [the rescript] for you."

When the rescript had been read aloud, T'aego picked up the whisk and said: "Is there anyone who is truly worthy of the vehicle of the school that has come down from antiquity? All the scriptures of the twelve-part canon of the five teachings and three vehicles are just piss left behind by an old barbarian. The buddhas and patriarchs were just guys talking about a dream in a dream. If you discuss them by making up reasons, you bury the vehicle of the school. If you discuss them in terms of conventional truth, you are turning your back on the former sages. This way won't do, otherwise won't do, 'won't do' also won't do. If you are a legitimate patchrobed monk, you can see it beyond all the permutations of affirmation and denial."

After answering questions, T'aego held up his staff horizontally and said: "All the buddhas of past, present, and future are Thus. All the generations of enlightened teachers are Thus. If it were not for our monarch's invitation, I would never explain fully this way.

"If the monarch and his high ministers can believe like this at this point, they will attract the protection of the buddhas and bring down the blessings of the devas. The monarch of the realm will live forever, with the warp and woof of cultural refinement and military might to assist his kingly enterprise of civilizing [the people]. The worthy ministers and high officials will extend their lives and their tenure in office. The transformative influence will reach the common people, so that worthy people will be found everywhere. All supernatural threats will dissipate even before they become manifest. Treason and rebellion will keep out of sight. Heaven and Earth will work their transformations even more, sun and moon will be even brighter, mountains and rivers will be even more solid, and the altars of earth and grain [emblematic of state and society] will flourish again. With timely rain and timely sunshine, the hundred grains will grow and the myriads of common people will be happy. Lucky unicorns and phoenixes resplendent with many colors will vie to offer auspicious signs in response [to your virtuous rule].

"If you are this way, then you are acting in accord with the sayings of the worthy sages of previous dynasties. If you believe in Buddha and submit to Heaven, then naturally you will succeed in making the nation great.

"Directed down, words get long: leave it to the staff! Again I have explained it clearly for the King, the Princess, the Queen, the Great Ministers, Generals, and Inner and Outer Officials."

T'aego brandished the staff once, held it up, and said: "Since this staff has no consciousness, how could there be right and wrong? I ask Your Majesty and the Great Ministers to collect your minds well and listen. Don't let it leak away."

He brandished the staff again and said: "If you're stuck in thinking what to do, you won't accomplish the noble task."

He brandished the staff again and said: "[Those in power who act] with complete public-spirited fairness without any private biases are protected and remembered by Heaven."

He brandished the staff again and said: "If they honor Buddha and stand in awe of Heaven, everyone will be safe and secure."

He brandished the staff again and said: "If they act contrary to this, [the consequences will be so dire that] though I have a mouth, it is hard to speak about it."

He brandished the staff again and said: "If the sage lord has a fit of anger, it thunders the same through millions of people's hearts." Then T'aego brandished the staff one more time and put it across his shoulder.

[The end of the scene was not recorded.]

[Later in the same session] T'aego again held up his staff and said: "In the old days on Sosol Mountain, I did not explain anything to people at all. Today in Locana Hall again there is nothing for me to say to people. I have received the benevolence of the state to no purpose: I lack the virtue to repay it in the least.

"I just keep busy like this mixing socially with idle spirits and wild demons, phantasmagorical ghosts and monsters.

All I hear are schemes for gain, which engender false thoughts and erroneous conceptions. As they make such calculations about the fickle, evanescent world, people's attempts to deal with it do not allow them a moment's rest. Isn't this caused by past deeds?"

T'aego brandished his staff and said: "This phony! Why is he rebuking himself?"

[Noting the occasion] T'aego said: "I have been invited to the royal palace and have ascended on high to this jewel seat. In the assembly of humans and devas, it is good to ask about the Path and good to ask about Zen. This is the ideal pattern, but in fact it is not so.

"This month the cold has already retreated and the morning sun shines victorious. This is our Great Lord ascending to the Bright Hall. There is no place that his flying intellect and swift illumination do not reach.

"To spread good order and employ humane considerations is the great policy of those who act as kings. When there are major events for the nation, they should rely on the power of the Buddha Dharma to secure themselves from false moves. Thus they must first set right their dealings with the Buddha Dharma. They must reward those who have the Path and act as patrons of Buddhist monasteries, leading their congregations in scrupulous practice, and bringing blessings on the families of the land. This is the way the Former Kings carried out the Dharma. This is the starting point for Kingly Government.

"The reason to leave home for the Path is not to seek fame or profit; it is not to make plans for a place to stay, clothes to wear, or food to eat; it is not to seek people's respect and acclaim. [Leavers of home] gladly keep discipline; they wear poor clothes and eat poor food; they hide away in the mountain valleys and have no expectations for their present bodies: this can be called the conduct of those who leave home to study the Path. People today are not only self-seeking, they take advantage of the power of others for their seeking. I cannot do anything about them."

T'aego brandished his staff and said: "Tigers do not eat animals with stripes, for fear of injuring their own kind."

T'aego also said: "Among the common people, there are indeed those loyal to the lord and filial to their parents, those who possess talent and virtue. Though they may be abandoned among the weeds, they still have concerns for the trend of the times, concerns for the nation, and are intent on saving the world and its people. Although I am stupid and unworthy, because I could not bear to be silent in the face of so many concerns, I have been introduced in the highest circles [as a Zen teacher].

"If [those in power] rewarded the worthy and the good and punished the wicked and the deceitful, who would not be loyal? Who would not be filial? Who would be without the Path? Who wouldn't study? Who wouldn't cultivate his own virtue?

"Nevertheless, if there is anyone here with the strength to uproot mountains and the energy to top the world, let him come forward and fight along with me. Let us sacrifice our bodies for the nation, and accomplish the great enterprise. This is not only for great nobles. If there are no such people here, then the old monk T'aego goes off to serve in the border forts by himself with a single horse and spear.

"But tell me, though I do go off, what is the one phrase that accomplishes the great enterprise?" After a long silence, T'aego said: "Holding the peerless sword crosswise, the true imperative whole: in the universe of Great Peace, cutting down stubborn stupidity." Then he brandished his staff twice.

8. RETURNING HOME TO THREE CORNERS MOUNTAIN

When he reached the temple gate, T'aego said: "I never left this gate in the old days and I am not entering it today. Nor is there any place within it to stay. Where will all of you go to see where I wander at play?" He brandished the staff.

After a long silence, T'aego said: "On the northern ridge, idle flowers red as brocade. In front of the mountain stream, flowing water green as indigo-plants."

9. ENTRY INTO PHOENIX CLIFF ZEN TEMPLE ON MOUNT HUIYANG

When he reached the temple gate, T'aego said: "All the buddhas of the past, present and future all come in and go out through this gate. But tell me, today am I going out or coming in? I am neither going out nor coming in: what is the principle of this?" He brandished the staff three times.

10. ENTRY INTO PRECIOUS FOREST ZEN TEMPLE ON MOUNT KAJI

When he arrived at the temple gate, T'aego said: "Old Shakyamuni said, 'I entrust this Dharma gate of mine to the rulers of states and their great ministers.' These are true words! Today I have come with a large group: we started out from Mount Huiyang and finally we have ended up before the gate of Mount Kaji, over three hundred miles away. We were on the road fourteen days. We proceeded south day after day and encountered no trouble on the road. Wherever we went it was the universal gate of perfect penetration: the way opened before us, all thanks to the protection and aid and benevolent power of the King and his ministers."

T'aego called out to the great assembly: "We have arrived, but how can we advance and repay such profound benevolence from above?" He brandished his staff and said: "The sound of the rushing stream is most intimate. The colors of the mountains are like it too."

At the buddha shrine T'aego said: "The ancient buddha Zhaozhou said, 'I don't like to hear even the word *buddha*.' I am not this way. I don't like the one who doesn't like it. 'In the old days I was you, today you are me.' Then he lit incense and bowed in homage.

At the abbot's room T'aego said: "To melt down ordinary people and refine them into sages, we employ the forge and bellows of heaven. But tell me, today, who can stand up to the sharp point? Bah!"

11. ENTRY INTO SHINING SOURCE ZEN TEMPLE ON MOUNT CHASSI

At the temple gate T'aego said: "The whole world is the gate to liberation. Do all of you see? If you do not see, I will bravely explain it to you." Then he brandished the staff and said: "The gate to liberation is wide open. Don't hesitate. Come along with me." Then he went through the gate.

At the abbot's room he said: "Here is a good room for the king of emptiness. In the old days it was called Lucky Cloud Cave. Nowadays a pure impoverished man of the path lives here. Buddhas and patriarchs may come, but he will not meet with them. Clear-eyed patchrobed monks cannot approach him. But tell me, who can instantly cut him off? Spreading the teaching according to the buddha, receiving beings according to their potentials. Bah—what idle words!"

T'aego went up the teaching hall, held his staff crosswise, and said: "Specks of white, traces of blue, strips of red, bands of empty space; the buddhas of the past have dwelt like this, the buddhas of the present are dwelling like this, the buddhas of the future will dwell like this. When I extol them like this, it is already sleeptalk. Why are all of you standing there asleep?"

Then T'aego brandished the staff three times and left the teacher's seat.

12. HOW TO MEDITATE WITH ZEN CASES

T'aego taught the assembly by citing [a public case]: "A monk asked Zhaozhou if a dog has buddha nature or not. Zhaozhou said, 'No.'

"This word *No* is like a pellet of alchemical cinnabar: touch iron with it and the iron turns to gold. As soon as his word *No* is mentioned, the face of all the buddhas of past, present, and future is revealed. Are all of you willing to accept it or not?

"If you cannot accept this with certainty, you should put down your body and mind at this point of great doubt, as if you were hanging from a cliff miles high. Do not calculate or assess: be like the person who has died the Great Death. Abandon all thoughts of what to do and how to act.

"Just bring up the word *No* all by itself. Twenty-four hours a day, in the midst of whatever your are doing, just take this meditation saying as the root of life. Always be attentive: examine it all the time. Put your attention on the saying and stick it in front of your eyes. Be like a hen sitting on her eggs to make sure they stay warm. Be like a cat waiting to catch a mouse. Body and mind do not move, and the eye doesn't leave [the objective] even for a moment. Do not be aware of body and mind, of existence and nonexistence. In the mind's eye hold the meditation saying in place.

"Just go on like this, more and more alert and clear, investigating closely, like an infant thinking of its mother, like someone hungry longing for food, like someone thirsty thinking of water. Rest but do not stop: contemplate more and more deeply. This is by no means a contrived state of mind [we aim for here].

"If you can truly function like this, then you arrive at the place of saving power. This is also the place of gaining power. The meditation point spontaneously becomes pure and ripe, and fuses everything into one. Body and mind are suddenly empty, fused solid and motionless: mind has nowhere to go.

"At this point, there's just you yourself. If you allow thoughts of otherness to arise, then you are sure to be deluded by the reflections [of the one reality]. Above all, be sure not to allow the least extraneous thought that sets it apart from you. You should turn around and look to see what *His* face, the face of reality, is.

"Once again: what did Zhaozhou mean when he said 'No'? If you can smash ignorance under [the impact of] this word [*No*], then you are like a man drinking water who knows for himself whether it is cool or warm. If you cannot penetrate through, then apply more energy.

"You must make [your attention on] the meditation point continuous without a break. No matter whether you have doubts or not, no matter whether there is an interesting flavor or not, at the point of great doubt, keep your attention on the meditation saying. Moment to moment with attention undimmed, keep extending and prolonging it. When walking, just be like this. When sitting, just be like this. Just be like this at mealtimes and when you are talking to people. Be like this in all that you do whether moving or still, and nothing will not be accomplished.

"Do all of you recognize the profound generosity of the four forms of benevolence [the benevolence of parents, of the teacher, of the king, of donors]? Do all of you recognize the ugly body made of the four elements [for what it is], as it decays from moment to moment? Do you realize that your very life [is only certain] from breath to breath?

"Have you met buddhas and enlightened teachers appearing in the world? Have you been born to hear of the vehicle of the supreme school? Having heard of this supreme vehicle, do you feel how rare it is [to encounter such a teaching]? Do you avoid miscellaneous talk in the monks' hall to contemplate the recorded sayings [of the former Zen teachers]? Do you depart from the discipline you keep in the monks' hall?

"Whether walking, sitting, standing, or lying down, do you investigate the meditation saying twenty-four hours a day without interruption? Do you investigate it at mealtimes? Do you lose awareness of it when you are talking to people? Is the meditation saying there when you are upset and harried? Are you chatting with the one next to you in the meditation hall? Don't you always talk idly and loosely with other people making judgments of right and wrong? Do you [fulfill the Buddhist admonition] 'don't notice others' mistakes, don't talk of others' faults'? Do you apply effort all the time and constantly advance?

"When you see and sense and know, are you always perfectly clear and fused into one whole? When you arrive at a good time, do you turn back and contemplate yourself? How can your own face catch Zhaozhou? When Zhaozhou said 'No,' what did he mean? Can you continue the buddhas' life of wisdom in this life?

"Do the monks of the various ranks honor and respect each other? When they arise from sitting and are at ease, are they mindful of the pains of hell?

"This is the truth that people who come to grips with Zen check out in their daily activities. Those who really study Zen must learn like this.

"I offer you the pattern according to your questions. Everyone should say something so we can see [where you're at]. If you cannot utter some words, we cannot let you go."

13. THE MIND-GROUND

At the behest of the King, T'aego gave a brief outline of the basic principles of Zen:

"Here with me, there is basically no dharma at all, so how could there be words? Nevertheless, there cannot be no answer. The King of the nation has again requested me to talk about the wordless, to talk directly about the mind-ground.

"There is something bright and clear, without falsity, without biases, tranquil and unmoving, possessed of vast consciousness, fundamentally without birth and death and discrimination, without names and forms and words. It engulfs space and covers all of heaven and earth, all of form and sound, and is equipped to function.

"If we speak of its essence, it is so vast it embraces everything, so that nothing is outside of it. If we speak about its function, then it goes beyond the abilities of the samadhi of the spiritual powers of the wisdoms numerous as the dusts in the buddha-lands: it is at once hidden and manifest, sovereign and free in all directions, with great spiritual powers. Even great sages cannot get to the end of it.

"This one thing is always with each and every person. Whether you move or not, whenever you encounter circumstances and objects, it is always very obvious and clear, clear everywhere, revealed in everything. It is quietly shining in all activities. As an expedient, it is called Mind. It is also called the Path, and the king of the myriad dharmas, and Buddha. Buddha said that whether walking, sitting, or lying down, we are always within it. Even Yao and Shun said: 'Holding faithfully to the mean, without contrived activity, everything under heaven is well ordered.' Weren't Yao and Shun sages? Weren't the buddhas and enlightened teachers special people? They simply managed to illuminate This Mind.

"Therefore, since antiquity, the buddhas and enlightened teachers have never established words and texts [as sacred]: they just transmitted Mind with Mind, without any other separate teaching. If there is some other teaching outside This Mind, this is a deluded theory, not the words of Buddha. Thus, when we use the name Mind, it is not the ordinary person's mind that falsely engenders discrimination: rather, it is the silent and motionless Mind in each person.

"People cannot preserve this inherent Mind for themselves. Unwittingly they make false moves and are suddenly thrown into confusion by the wind of objects: they are buried in sensory experiences, which arise and disappear again and again. They falsely create the karmic suffering of endless birth and death. Therefore, the buddhas and enlightened teachers and sages appeared in the world by the power of their past [bodhisattva] vows. They use great compassion and directly point out that the human mind is inherently enlightened, and they enable people to awaken to the mind-buddha.

"Your Majesty must contemplate his own inherent mind. During lulls in the myriad functions of state, Your Majesty should sit upright in the palace, without thinking of good and evil at all, abandoning at once all phenomena of body and mind, just like a golden statue of Buddha. Then the false thinking of birth and destruction is totally obliterated, and the obliterating is obliterated, in an instant the mind-ground is quiet and motionless, with nothing to rest on. Body and mind are suddenly empty: it's like leaning on the void. All that appears here is total clarity and illumination.

"At this moment, you should look carefully at your original face before your father and mother were born. As soon as it is brought up, you awaken to it: then, like a person drinking water, you know yourself whether it is cool or warm. It cannot be described or explained to anyone else. It's just a luminous awareness covering heaven and earth.

"When the realm I've just talked about spontaneously appears before you, you will have no doubts about birth and death, you will have no doubts about the sayings of the buddhas and enlightened teachers—indeed, you will have met the buddhas and enlightened teachers. This is the wonder transmitted from 'father' to 'son' by the buddhas and enlightened teachers since antiquity. You must make it your concern: be careful not to neglect it. Be like this even when attending to affairs of state and working for the renovation of the people. Use this Path also to be alert to all events and to encourage all your ministers and common subjects to share together in the uncontrived inner truth and enjoy Great Peace. Then the buddhas and nagas and devas are sure to rejoice and extend supernatural aid [to the monarch] in ruling the country.

"Not only in this life, but over many lifetimes, Your Majesty has encountered buddhas and sages: he has planted a deep basis for transcendent wisdom in this vehicle of the highest school. By the power of our fundamental vows, today I take joy in discussing this truth with Your Majesty in a spontaneous and uncontrived way, as if poking around for a spark in last night's fire. To accomplish the great matter, you must have no doubts.

"Those of the nation's people blessed with wisdom will obey the King's will and respect him as if he were Buddha. Their inner joy will show on their faces as they proclaim, 'Our Lord is the Buddha-Mind King' and praise him without end. Such people are surely those who in the past planted the roots of goodness along with His Majesty, so that they have not matured.

"As for those who hear and give rise to doubts, or those who have not heard [of the King's role as the protector of Buddhism], they are scarcely worth talking about."

14. THIS WORK IS VERY SUBTLE

[Answer to a letter from O Su, Layman Pangsan]

I have been unable, due to sickness brought on by karma, to go to the city to meet with you. Though I am out in the country, in reality not a day goes by that I don't visit you. Is that all right with you?

Today unexpectedly I got your letter. I already knew that you are secure in your activities and have your heart set on this matter. You are making the activities of the Path your daily activities. I am very happy for you. In your letter you say that you are observing the meditation saying as thought arises instantaneously moment after moment. This work is very subtle. An ancient worthy said: "Do not fear the instantaneous arising of thought: just be afraid you will be slow to awaken." It is also said: "If you awaken as thoughts arise, having awakened to them, they are not there." It is also said: "From moment to moment of thought, grasping at all the various objects; mind-moment to mind-moment, forever cutting off all discrimination." These sayings are all clues by adepts to help people. Old

Pang said: "Just vow to empty all that exists; do not make real, things that do not exist."

I invite you to distinguish religious from worldly and assess their gains and losses, so that you may arrive at the ultimate extreme of good fortune.

In the letter I received from you, the sense of invitation was most urgent; the repetitive verbiage, the "creeping vines," the thoughts arising and disappearing—we call this birth and death. Right in the midst of birth and death, you must use all your strength to bring up the meditation saying. When [your attention on] the meditation saying is pure and unified, the arising and disappearing ends. The end of arising and disappearing is called stillness. To be in the midst of stillness without the meditation saying is called indeterminacy. To be mindful of the meditation saying amidst the stillness is called spiritual awareness. This empty and still spiritual awareness is indestructible and uncontaminated. If you can work like this [at the Buddhist Path], success will come soon.

Your body and mind and the meditation will become fused into one whole. You have no dependencies and your mind is not headed anywhere. At this time, there will only be you. If you think thoughts of otherness, then you are sure to be deluded by the reflections.

Constantly check out [the meditation saying]: go for days and days without a break.

If you can go by the Dharma for three days without a break, with motion and stillness, speech and silence, as one suchness, and the meditation saying constantly appearing before you, this is still like moonlight on the bank of a swift stream. You touch it but it doesn't disperse, you push it but it doesn't go away, you sweep it away but it isn't lost. Being awake and being asleep are one suchness. The time of great enlightenment is near.

When you reach this juncture, do not seek rationalizations from people, and do not talk with idlers. Just be like an ignorant mute twenty-four hours a day, whether walking, sitting, standing, or lying down. Abandon body and mind: be like a dead person. Don't let the inside out and don't let the outside in. To forget the meditation saying here would be a great mistake. Before the great doubt is shattered, do not by any means forget the meditation saying.

If you do just as I say, and really reach this stage, then suddenly ignorance will shatter, and you will empty through in great enlightenment. After you are enlightened, you must see a legitimate expert of the Zen school, to make the final selections [for you] and lead you to the ultimate. If [people at this stage] do not see a teacher, ten times out of ten they will become demons. I send my prayers.

15. CONTEMPLATING "NO"

[To Chang Hae, Layman Mugye]

A monk asked Zhaozhou: "Does a dog have buddha-nature or not?" Zhaozhou said: "No." This word *No* is not the *No* of existence and one existence. It is not the *No* of true nothingness. Ultimately, what is it?

When you arrive here, you must abandon all with your whole body, not doing anything, not doing not-doing-any-thing. Go straight to the empty and free and vast, with no pondering what to think. The previous thought is already extinct, the following thought does not arise, the present thought is itself empty. You do not hold to emptiness, and you forget you are not holding on. You do not reify this forgetting: you escape from not reifying and the escape too is not kept. When you reach such a time, there's just a spiritual light that's clearly aware and totally still, appearing as a lofty presence.

Do not wrongly give birth to interpretations: just bring up the meditation saying twenty-four hours a day, what-ever you are doing. Do not be oblivious of it for a moment: diligently come to grips with it and study it in fine detail. If you keep studying like this, pulling it back and forth, when you reach the proper time, you better look back most carefully and see what Zhaozhou's *No* means. When you are [unable to turn back] like a rat going into a [hollow] horn, then views are cut off.

When those of sharp faculties get here, they empty through and smash the lacquer bucket [of ignorance] and capture and defeat Zhaozhou. They have no more doubts about the sayings of the world's [enlightened] people.

Even if you are awakened like this, do not speak of it in front of people without wisdom. You must go see a legitimate teacher of the school.

16. THE ORIGINAL FACE

[To the degree-holder Ch'oe]

You ask: "What was my original face before my father and mother were born?" If you can understand completely as soon as it is mentioned, then you're through. If not, then you should be continuously mindful [of this question] twenty-four hours a day, without letting your mind ignore it, whatever you are doing. Be like a chicken guarding an egg, like a cat stalking a mouse. If you can keep on like this, within three to seven days you are sure to get some measure of accord [with the inner meaning of the question].

This road is the starting point to the direct illumination of the Former Kings. As you discuss the skill in means here, you will think: "My physical body, composed of the four elements, was obviously born from my father and mother. At some unspecified time, it is sure to decompose. What was my original face before my father and mother were born?"

Come to grips with this without falling into oblivion thousands and thousands of times. If you are like this without interruption, then naturally your work will become pure and ripe and your body and mind will be clear and content, like the crisp air of autumn.

When they get there, those of sharp faculties open through in great enlightenment. Like people drinking water, they know for themselves whether it is cool or warm: all they can do is accept it for themselves in total clarity and comprehension. Only then can you be sure of [the truth of] the saying: "When awareness is exhausted and the body has nothing to depend on: only then do you see the original person."

17. WHO'S ASKING?

[To Layman Saje]

Knowing that impermanence is swift, and birth and death is an important matter, you have come specially to ask about the Path. This is indeed the conduct of a real man.

Still: who is the one who recognizes impermanence and birth and death like this? And who is the one who has come specially to ask about the Path? If you can discern truly here, Layman, then, as we say, "The visage is unique and wondrous: the light shines on the ten directions. We have just made an offering: now we return to our kin."

Nevertheless: do not stop your potential and linger in thought over these four lines using your conceptual mind and inbred biases. If you do, the more you explain, the farther away you get. Thus it is better to study the living phrase.

Haven't you read [this case]? A monk asked Zhaozhou, "Does a dog have a buddha-nature or not?" Zhaozhou said, "No." This "No" is not the *No* of existence and nonexistence, nor is it the *No* of real nothingness. But tell me, in the end, what truth is it? If you understood as soon as it is brought up, then you're done. If you hesitate in doubt, unable to break through, then you must raise the word *No* to study and observe right where your doubt does not break. Whether walking, standing, sitting or lying down, twenty-four hours a day, always be aware of it. Just go on studying this way and carefully contemplating *No*.

If you penetrate through, then you immediately meet Zhaozhou. At that point, you must visit a legitimate teacher of the Zen school. Get going!

18. OUTLINE OF ESSENTIALS FOR RECITING THE BUDDHA-NAME

[To Layman Nagam]

"Amitabha Buddha" is Sanskrit: in our language it means "Buddha of Infinite Life." The word *buddha* is also Sanskrit: in our language it means "enlightened one."

The fact is that the fundamental nature of each and every person contains a great spiritual awareness. It is fundamentally without birth and death. It extends through ancient and modern, spiritually alive and illuminated, undefiled, wondrous, sovereign in peace and bliss. Is this not the Buddha of Infinite Life?

Thus it is said: "To illuminate this mind is called being a buddha. To speak of this mind is called the scriptural teachings." The whole great canon of scriptural teachings spoken by Buddha are expedient means to point out the inherent enlightened nature of all people. Although the expedient means are many, in essence they teach of the Pure Land of mind and the Amitabha of inherent nature. If mind is pure, then the buddha-land is pure. If reality-nature appears, then the buddha-body appears. This is precisely what [the scriptural teachings] mean.

The pure, wondrous *dharmakaya* of Amitabha Buddha is everywhere in the mind-ground of all sentient beings. Thus it is said: "Mind, buddhas, sentient beings—these three are no different." It is also said: "Mind is buddha, buddha is mind. Outside of mind there is no buddha, outside of buddha there is no mind."

If you genuinely recite the buddha-name, you are just invoking the Amitabha of your own inherent nature. Twenty-four hours a day, whatever you are doing, take the words "Amitabha Buddha" and stick them before your mind's eye. Let your mind's eye and the buddha-name become fused into one whole, until this continues undimmed from mind-moment to mind-moment. Sometimes turn back and contemplate closely on an intimate level who the one reciting is.

After a long period of work, suddenly in an instant mind and thoughts are cut off, and Amitabha Buddha's real body will appear before you as a lofty presence. Only then will you be sure about the saying "The one who has never moved is Buddha."

19. WHO IS RECITING THE BUDDHA-NAME?

[To Layman Paek Ch'ung]

Buddha said: "Beyond thousands of millions of buddha-lands, there is a land called Ultimate Bliss. This land has a buddha, called Amitabha. Now he appears teaching the Dharma . . ." In these words of Buddha there is a profound intimate esoteric meaning. Do you recognize it or not, Layman?

Put Amitabha Buddha's name in your mind: be undimmed and mindful of it all the time, moment to moment without a break. Come to grips with it and contemplate it earnestly. When your thoughts and ideas are exhausted, then turn back and observe: who is the one mindful of the buddha-name? Also observe: who is the one who can observe back this way?

Give this close detailed study: come to grips with it on an intimate level. Suddenly this mind is cut off, and the Amitabha of inherent nature appears before you as a grand presence. Work hard on it!

20. MAKE A CLEAN BREAK

[To Zen man Tang]

Those in ancient times who left home sensed the special reality of this matter [of enlightenment] as soon as they heard of it: they became brave and bold and advanced directly, vowing not to retreat. Thus the life of wisdom has not been cut off, and the lamp of mind has not come to an end: the proper people have not been lacking in the gate of the buddhas and ancestral teachers.

Ten out of ten of those who leave home these days obstruct themselves by self-deprecation. People are very lazy: they push this matter [of enlightenment] up on high to the realm of the sages, and are content to be inferior. It seems that they do not believe that the physical body is [as fleeting] as the morning dews, and life [ends] as quickly as the last rays of sunlight in the west. Sometimes they work hard, sometimes they are lazy: the things they like to do are all the karmic basis for the three mires. They indulge their feelings of joy, anger, sorrow, fear, love, hate, and desire and so bring about karma of body, mouth and mind. Thus, though it is easy to create false karma, later on the mountain of swords, in the forest of blades, in the boiling cauldrons [of hell], it will be very difficult to bear the sufferings of the karmic retribution.

Since you have left home, what better than to generate a brave and bold mind today, while everything is prepared, and the time is favorable, and decisively establish a fixed intent. Put aside your feelings and thoughts: make a clean break. Study this matter [of enlightenment]. The moment you break through to enlightenment, birth and death are immediately cut off. No more will you doubt the tongues of all the world's people. Buddhas and patriarchs will not be able to do anything about you. Isn't this the ultimate unconcerned peace and bliss?

21. BE INTENT

[To Zen man Chin]

Now that you have left home, you must establish the intent of a great man and unfurl a brave and bold mind. Believe deeply that impermanence is swift and the matter of birth and death is important. Whether walking, standing, sit-

ting, or lying down, at all times stay clearly aware of this.
Study it earnestly and carefully. Be like a person who has
fallen into a thousand-foot-deep well, who thinks and pon-
ders ten thousand times, with the sole intention of seeking
a way out. [With this attitude], before too long you are sure
to have some measure of accord [with the Dharma]. You
are sure to succeed if you work like this: otherwise, the
Buddha Dharma would have no spiritual effectiveness.

In the old days Xiangyan heard a knock on bamboo and
awakened to the Path; Lingyun saw a peach blossom and
was enlightened to Mind. If a person acts like this, being
alert and clear twenty-four hours a day whether walking,
standing, sitting, or lying down, and not dimming mindfulness of this matter [of enlightenment], but keeping it
pure and unified and unmixed, if he acts this way when
moving or still, when talking or silent, with wakefulness
and sleep as one suchness, then when hearing sound and
seeing form, there is sure to be [enlightenment as with]
Xiangyan and Lingyun.

People who study Zen must examine and check themselves at all times to see whether or not their efforts match
the ancients. If there are deficiencies, rebuke yourself
again and again, and strengthen your resolve to be enlightened. From hour to hour and moment to moment, do not
think at all: at just such a time, what is our original face
from before our fathers and mothers were born? Be mindful of this all the time and carefully and intently come to
grips with it. Suddenly your mind has nowhere to go, and
becomes one whole [with reality]. When those with sharp
faculties get here, they smash their ignorance: after that
they must see a legitimate Zen teacher.

22. BEYOND WORDS

[To Zen man Ui]

Our original teacher Buddha, the World Honored One,
said to Ananda: "Even if you memorized the sutras of the

tathagatas of past, present, and future, this is not as good as one day's cultivation of stainless learning." Such true, frank words in this solid statement!

The wondrous truth handed down by all the buddhas and ancestral teachers does not lie in written or spoken words. Nevertheless, out of great compassion, the enlightened ones had no choice as they responded to people's potentials but to use written and spoken words. The written and spoken words were specially directed toward medium and lower potentials, using these expedient means to directly indicate the mind-ground. But in general people studying Buddhism take these expedients as real and do not relinquish them. Isn't this a great disease? They are like the prodigal son, who has left his father to go wandering, who sojourns in travelers' inns which he falsely considers to be his own home. Not only has the prodigal son lost his home, but when will he ever find his way back? Alas, what a great pity for those who hold to the pointing finger as the moon.

But you are not like this now. You know for certain that the words of the buddhas and ancestral teachers were all expedient means for indicating the mind-ground. You have made a clean break with your former studies of interpreting words. You should study the mind-ground: you must accomplish the great work in one life. Then you can cut off birth and death and repay the fourfold benevolence [of parents, teachers, the ruler and the donors]. The human mind-ground is very subtle and wondrous. It cannot be understood with words or grasped with thought or penetrated with silence.

Just keep this matter before you at all times, and above all do not [let your attention to it] dim. When you have naturally become one [with the mind-ground], you reach the place where you know nothing, understand nothing. Do not try to think what it is, just be completely alert and clear, and be able to continue this at all times whatever you are doing, whether moving or still, talking or silent. Once you get power, then there will be a good season. But you must not talk about this in front of people with no wisdom.

After this you must see a legitimate teacher of the school for [a process of] intimate level selection [to help you advance further]. This is a life's work for great men.

23. FACING INFINITY

[Answer to Elder Suk of Chamdang]

I have respectfully received the solicitous letter of the Zen elder in charge of the monks at Kaech'on Hall.

In it you said: "Due to old age and sickness, I have a bit of the will [for enlightenment] that comes with cutting grief. I seek a turning word to be my last sustenance."

These are not at all useless words! I too have felt grief. Ancient and modern, when it comes to the last day of the last month, the world's people take the attitude that the old year has already ended, but the new year is arriving, so they just celebrate and congratulate each other on this, to suit their human sentiments. Since you are one among them, Zen Elder, you too use this occasion to take alarm about the flow of time, and so you have come out with genuinely true words.

Surely you know, Zen Elder, that your own spiritual illumination is magnificent and grand, totally naked and free, impossible to take hold of. How could there by any difference between ancient and modern or new and old in this? It is fundamentally without views of ordinary and sage, and unrelated to the falsity of birth and death. The ancients called it the "true person without position" but even this isn't accurate. What shall we call it now? The person drinks the water and knows for himself whether it's cool or warm. Please laugh once and see.

The ancient buddha Zhaozhou spoke the word *No* in order to open the eyes of all the patchrobed ones in the world. I wonder how many patchrobed ones' eyes there are in Kaech'on Hall? Right now, are they open? If there are any among them that are not yet opened, I give you a verse:

> Abandon the myriad starting points of concern:
> You must cross Zhaozhou's barrier.
> Study till you understand nothing:
> Then it is whole.
> If you go on directly like this,
> In an instant you will smash the mass of doubt.
> For the family business of the patchrobed ones,
> Act like this and you will be secure and at ease.
> The last day of the last month
> Also can be a pure meal.
> Exchanging greetings and congratulations:
> How can this compare with looking on in spontaneous
>   happiness?
> Only by walking barefoot on ice and snow
> Can you know the cold that pierces to the bone.
> Of course teachers are prepared in advance:
> I too am among them helping.

24. PICK UP THE SWORD OF WISDOM

[To Zen man Mon]

Since you have realized your mistake and abandoned fame and fortune, in this life you must repay the benevolence of the buddhas and ancestral teachers. If you now [linger in your preliminary achievement], when will you finally cut off the root of ignorance? You have already generated the resolve of a great man. Time and time again you must pick up the sword [of transcendent wisdom], the sword so sharp it cuts a hair blown across it. If you always act like this, what is there to disturb the inner truth from outside?

When you get to the end of the road and are facing an iron wall, thoughts linked to objects and false concerns are forever stilled. The effect is like pure white beams of moonlight penetrating ice. Gradually you reach the place where being awake and beings asleep are one suchness. Sense objects will cease and light will shine forth. When you get here, do not give rise to sadness or joy or interpretive knowledge. As soon as you produce interpretive knowledge, you lose the power of the achievement.

Just keep your attention [on the one suchness] and keep your eyes awake and alert. Again and again observe what form it has. Suddenly you will capture the barrier of the buddhas and ancestral teachers: it's just worth a laugh. After that you should seek out and study with true Zen teachers, who will take you by the nostrils and selectively lead you into the same stream of life.

25. DOUBT

[To Zen man So]

Buddha preached discipline, concentration, and wisdom to purify the realms of body, mouth, and mind. You should uphold pure discipline, not commit the misdeeds of body, mouth, and mind. From moment to moment, bring up Zhaozhou's *No.* You should never at any time let yourself become oblivious of this *No.* Keep this *No* before you at all times, whether you are walking or standing or sitting or lying down or going to the toilet or putting on clothes or eating food. Be like a cat stalking a rat or like a chicken guarding an egg. Do not become oblivious: just raise this *No.*

As you [keep your attention on] the meditation saying like this without a break, studying it and doubting it [and asking] why Zhaozhou said *No,* before you break through the doubt, your mind feels vexed. This is precisely when you should bring up this meditation saying. When continuous correct mindfulness of the meditation saying is achieved, you should keep studying again and again in fine detail as you observe the meditation saying. Your doubt and the meditation saying fuse into one whole. Whether moving or still, speaking or silent, constantly bring up this *No.* Gradually you arrive at the time when being awake and being asleep are one suchness. Just do not let the meditation saying and the mind separate.

When your doubting reaches the place where sentiments are cut off and mind is forgotten, then the golden raven flies through the sky at midnight [true *yang*, inherent enlightened perception emerges at the proper moment.] When this happens, you should not feel happy or sad: you must visit a genuine Zen teacher to resolve your doubts forever.

26. IN THIS LIFETIME

[To Zen man Ka]

I urge you to develop the resolve of a great man, and pay back the benevolence of your teacher in this lifetime. At present the Correct Dharma is about to decline. To perpetuate the lamp of illumination and deliver people from delusion, to smash through the net of the many perversities of the world, you must meet with a clear-eyed man. Do not put gold dust in your eyes. Suddenly pluck out the root of affliction from the mind-ground. Sail across the ocean of suffering forever in the boat of transcendent wisdom. Let your work in benefiting yourself and benefiting others be renewed every day. The work of a great man is just like this. You should vow not to treat this truth casually.

27. FOR YOUR PARENTS' SAKE

[To Zen man Sang]

When you first came to me to be ordained a monk, both your parents were sad and cried. The benevolent love of father and mother is heavier than a mountain. When they let you leave home, how could they feel good about it?

Recognizing such benevolence on the part of your parents, you should practice scrupulously and advance energetically with a sense of great urgency. If you seek fame and fortune and put aside actual practice of the Path, then this is the practice of uninterrupted black karma.

What human being lives forever? It's a pity, but this fleeting life [might be gone between the time] you breathe in and breathe out. Therefore our honored teacher [Shakyamuni Buddha] forsook his throne and left the royal city; he went into the mountains and practiced austerities for six years. Spiders spun their webs on his eyebrows and sparrows nested on his shoulders [as he sat in contemplation]: in a loincloth of reeds he was free and at ease. Did Buddha suffer in the least from the name and fame disorder?

Since you are now learning this conduct from a teacher, your parents and all your relations are sure to be born in heaven. If you disobey your teacher's instructions, and become just an [imitation monk], a layman without hair, then you will drag your teacher and your relatives along with you into uninterrupted hell.

28. ZEN FOR A LADY

[To the princess of Ansan Commandery]

To study Zen you must penetrate through the barrier of the ancestral teachers. To learn the Path you must come to the end of the road of mind. When the road of mind is cut off, the whole body appears. It's like a person drinking water: she knows for herself whether it's cool or warm.

When you reach this stage, do not ask just anyone about it: you must join a real Zen teacher and show her how your mind is working.

29. RIGHT WHERE YOU STAND

[To Zen man Yu]

Since you have come to me for ordination, in this life you must repay the profound benevolence of parents, teachers, the monarch, and donors. Without the power of energetic progress in cultivating practice, what will you use to illuminate Mind and penetrate infinity?

[To the Japanese Zen man Jisho]

The white sun rises in Japan
I invite you to see it right
Look back with clear comprehension
Right where you stand is the site of enlightenment

[to Zen man Ui]

People of great wisdom ancient and modern
Recognize the illusory body [for what it is] from
    moment to moment
Recognizing the illusory, they are detached from the
    illusory
Right there appears the fundamental reality

30. SONG OF T'AEGO HERMITAGE

I've lived in this hermitage how long I don't know
Deep and secret and without obstructions
Heaven and earth meet like box and cover: there's
    no turning toward or turning away
I do not stay in the east, west, south or north
The jewel tower and the jade palace do not stand
    opposite me
I do not take the guidelines of Bodhidharma as a
    model as I shine through eighty-four thousand
    gates
On That Side, beyond the clouds, the mountain is
    blue-green as jade
The white clouds on the mountain are whiter than
    white
From the spring on the mountain, drop after drop
Who knows how to see the face in the white clouds?
Clear skies and rain have their times—they're like
    lightning
Who knows how to listen to the sound of this spring?
It flows on without stopping through thousands and
    thousands of turns
The moment before thought is born is already wrong
To try to say anything further is embarrassing

I've gone through frost and gone through rain: how
    many springs and autumns?
Through what idle matter have I come to know
    Today?
Coarse I eat, fine I eat:
I let each and every one of you hurriedly eat
    Yunmen's cake and Zhaozhou's tea:
How do they compare to the flavorless food in my
    hermitage?
This is the old family style that's been there all along:
Who would dare tell you that it's special?
On the tip of a hair: T'aego Hermitage
Wide but not wide, narrow but not narrow
An endless array of lands is hidden here
Potential beyond measure colliding with heaven
The tathagatas of past, present and future do not
    understand
The generations of ancestral teachers cannot get away
Stupid and mute, the master [of the hermitage]
Acting upside-down and rebellious without any rules
Putting on the tattered cotton shirt of Qingzhou
In the shadow of the creeping vines, I lean on a sheer
    wall
Before my eyes, neither things nor people
Mornings and evenings empty I face the colors of the
    green mountain
Aloof and unconcerned I sing this song
The sound that came from the West is even more true
In the whole world, who can sing along in harmony?
[In the Zen transmission] as Spirit Peak and Shaoshi
    they clapped along
Who will take T'aego's no-string zither
To answer this hole-less flute that's here now?
Haven't you seen the ancient business in T'aego
    ["Ancient"] Hermitage?
It's just this one that's clear and aware right now
Hundreds of thousands of samadhis are within it
It benefits beings and responds to situations while
    always utterly still

I am not the only one living in this hermitage:
Countless buddhas and enlightened teachers share its
    style
I tell you for certain: have no doubts
Wisdom is hard to know: conceptual consciousness
    cannot fathom it
Turning the light around and reflecting back is still
    vague
Taking it up directly is still being struck on traces
To come forward to ask what it is, is a great error
Unmoving suchness is like an unknowing stone
Let it go without any false thinking
This is the great perfect enlightenment of the
    tathagatas
Over the ages, when has it ever gone out the gate?
For a little while it lingers on the present road
Originally this hermitage was not named T'aego
But for today we call it T'aego
All in one, one in many
We do not have to be in the one: we comprehend
    completely forever
It can be square and it can be round
Wherever it turns following the flow everything is
    awe-inspiring mystery
If you ask me about the scene on the mountain:
The wind in the pines is a lonesome lute, moonlight
    fills the river
Not "cultivating the Path," not "studying Zen"
Submerged in the water, its fire out, the stove has no
    smoke
Just *Him* passing by this way so exultant
How can you seek to be this way by employing a petty
    compartmentalized approach?
Pure to his bones, poor to his bones
For him to make a living, what's before the Primordial
    Buddha is there by itself
He comes at ease with ample praise for Taego's
    strange leanings
Riding backwards on an iron ox among humans and
    devas

A lad exhausting his tricks wherever his eye touches
He cannot be dragged back: in vain his eyelids are
    pierced
The ugliness and awkwardness in the hermitage are
    just like this
It's obvious—what need is there to repeat it?
After the dance is finished and he has returned to the
    triple terrace [of body, mind, and spirit]
As before the green mountain faces the forest spring

31. SHIWU'S NOTE ON T'AEGO

He is the elder of Mansu Zen Temple, which is in
Chunghung Zen Temple in the southern capital of Koryo.
His name is Po-u and his sobriquet is T'aego. Long since
he established his resolve for this one great matter. He has
done painful and hard meditative work: his perception has
penetrated through to liberation. He has cut off the road
of ideation and gone beyond thinking: he cannot be held
back by words and forms.

He wanted to hide away, so he built a hermitage on
Three Corners Mountain: he used his own name for it and
called it "T'aego" too. He is content with the Path and at
ease among the streams and rocks. He has written this
"Song of T'aego."

In the spring of 1346 he left his home and came to the
great capital [of the Yuan dynasty], not shrinking from the
efforts of the journey, seeking the traces [of Zen]. In the
seventh [lunar] month of 1347, he reached the stone hermitage on my mountain. For half a month we spoke of the
Path, silent and forgetful of everything else. I observed
that his conduct was effortlessly correct, and his words
were true and solid.

When he was about to leave, he took out this "Song of
T'aego" that he had previously written and showed it to
me. So I unrolled it by the pure window and read it appre-
ciatively: my old eyes were illuminated some more. I chant
his song and it is pure and generous, I savor his phrases

and they are carefree and profound. He has really attained the scene from before the empty eon. He cannot be compared with those these days who pile up sharp new nails [to imitate Zen language]. Thus his name [T'aego, "Great Ancient"] is no mistake. My pen leaps suddenly: unaware, I've written to the end of the page. I'll add a verse for him:

This hermitage was there first
Only then, the world
When the world crumbles
This hermitage will not be destroyed
The host inside the hermitage
Is present everywhere
The moon shines on the eternal void
The wind whistles through ten thousand openings

Eight month, seventh year of the Zhi Zheng era, *ding-hai* in the cycle of years [autumn, 1347 C.E.]

The old patch-robed one, Shiwu, who lives on Mount Xiawu in Huzhou, wrote this at age seventy-five.

32. SONG OF THE SAMADHI OF MIXED FLOWERS

Buddha's great extensive *Huayan Sutra:*
Whose words are these without a sound?
Our original teacher, old Gautama, a man of
    knowledge:
The realm he witnessed had endless layers of
    illumination
Vast and boundless, deep and broad, overwhelmingly
    awesome
Reaching everywhere, his perfect voice was like
    thunder
At the site of enlightenment he begins his exposition
In ocean seal samadhi he preaches without preaching
Who hears this? Who transmits this?
Manjusri and Samantabhadra [speak] with the
    tongues of great beings

But where did these two mahasattvas learn of this
      secret?
By deeply entering into this ocean of samadhis
Vairocana's body is hidden in samadhi
Why are Manjusri and Samatanbhadra so stupid?
They expose the family's ugliness to let outsiders
      know
Alas, how sad for people in the last age!
They search through texts and wear out their spirits
      in vain
If you hear [Buddha's teaching], he speaks from
      within infinite samadhi
If you turn your back on it, you will not learn what its
      basis is
This message is not just for the rich and noble
The thousand flowers and the hundred grasses all
      have spring within them
Profound people in later days who read the sutra
Do not ask the way to the great road of enlightenment
Stop! Stop! Why do you have to wander the south?
The site of enlightenment is right under your feet.
You should observe the old barbarian's silences
It cannot be taken up with words
Deeper than deep, darker than dark
Its wondrous functions are numberless as grains of
      sand and infinite
Ancient and modern [Buddhist teachers] have
      weighed petty people [and found]:
They cannot believe even simple direct
      demonstrations
Those who hear in vain without realization or wisdom
Are said to be like deaf mutes
They see but they cannot see fully
They hear but they cannot hear enough
People with this sort of mentality Buddha helped by
      gathering them together and sending them out
      [of the assemblies where he gave advanced
      teachings that they would misinterpret]
The samadhi work of the enlightened teacher of
      Mengshan

Burning incense, scattering flowers, alert and sharp
Paying homage to Buddha and chanting sutras, awake
    and sharp
From this alert wakefulness, you can do
    contemplation
Then gradually you achieve the inner truth of
    samadhi
Illuminated from samadhi to samadhi,
The reality-body of Vairocana appears perfect and
    complete
How fine it is: so many samadhis!
How good and fine is samadhi!
Complete from samadhi to samadhi,
Suddenly the Flower Treasury World appears
The Flower Treasury World is reduplicated endlessly,
    layer after layer
What I once heard and read, I now know for certain
Practicing it, wandering in it, personally experiencing
    it, I observed:
All the rivers and mountains in this world of suffering
The Unmoving Buddha in the middle of the Flower
    Treasury World
No fathers above, no grandsons below
Revolving smoothly, shining with light
Three times seven catties swallowed and spat out
Three bodies without a mouth
Eating up all the hundred herbs sweet and bitter
Always on the shore, always in midstream
In midstream the boat made of a single leaf is large
It carries all the people in ten thousand lands without
    obstruction
[The renowned Zen comrades] Hanshan and Shide
    were great enemies
Though busy, they never parted, but followed each
    other forever
Extreme intimacy reverts to estrangement in the sea
    of conflict
The boat is smashed and the pearls scattered
The fish and dragons and shrimp and crabs find
    these jewels

They hide them away on the floor of the deepest
    ocean
Sometimes walking, sometimes lying down,
    sometimes putting on clothes, sometimes eating,
We shamelessly receive this precious power
Ah, what a surprise! This is the way it is.
But I fear that the people of today [having heard of
    this] will intentionally seek it
This flower does not flow along with the mountain
    stream
How can we know the wanderings of the man of Qin
    in Peach Blossom Spring?
A sad person should not talk to sad people
If he talks to sad people, he saddens them further
Right now I personally take up the inexhaustible
    brush
To offer to the inexhaustible buddhas of the ten
    directions

33. SONG OF SPONTANEOUS JOY IN THE MOUNTAINS

Uncut whiskers, uncut hair
A fine ghost-headed demon!
Stupid and ignorant as a stone
Crude and dumb as a piece of wood
Wearing out straw sandals to study with enlightened
    teachers
Evil sounds and inane theories coming forth
    mechanically
La la lee, lee la la
Just to chant this tune I stop singing
The Great Yuan Son of Heaven is sagest of the sage:
He has bestowed on me the privilege of passing the
    days and months among rocky cliffs
There is no one to share my joy in the mountains
I'm only sorry my recounting of it is even more
    clumsy
I'd rather share spontaneous joy forever with the
    streams and rocks
I cannot let worldly people know of this joy

I only hope that the sagely life [of the emperor] lasts
ten thousand times ten thousand years
After that it will be possible for me not to worry
Amid the twists and turns of the cliffs and rushing
streams, the solitude is sweet
A small hermitage on a cliffside is enough to shelter
the body
It also lets the white clouds rest there
Haven't you seen the old monk T'aego's song?
In the song is inexhaustible joy
Spontaneous joy, spontaneous song—what doing is
there?
It's the uncontrived joy of the knowledge of destiny
in the heaven of bliss
Why the spontaneous song, the spontaneous joy?
I myself do not know what joy I'm enjoying
There's a meaning in this: do you recognize it or not?
Though it's hard for people to get hold of in daily
activities
In the depths of illumination intoxicated we play the
lute with no strings
Puhua would go into town shaking little bells
Budai was an idle monk completely without concerns
The wineshop in the red dust smells of dregs
The joy of the sages has been just like this ever since
ancient times
Leaving behind in vain the reverberations of an
empty name: how can there be silence?
Even those who can know it properly are hard to find
Even rarer are those who take joy in it and practice it
in action
You should observe T'aego's joy in this
The ascetic dances drunk
A crazy wind rises in the myriad channels
Spontaneous joy does not know the progression of the
seasons
I just watch the cliffside flowers open and fall

34. SONG OF THE HERMITAGE OF WHITE CLOUDS

On Freedom Mountain there are many white clouds
They accompany the moon on Freedom Mountain
    forever
Sometimes pure wind and many good things
Come to report that another mountain is even more
    special
Mindless, the white clouds spread over the great void
    of the sky
They are like a snowflake on a red-hot stove
They send rain to the four quarters without
    [discriminating between] this and that
Here all things are happy
Rejoicing in their instantaneous return, they come to
    this mountain
The mountain is sparkling with colors, the streams
    are murmuring
The ancient hermitage is still the same: it's not in the
    mists
On the perilous road covered with clouds the green
    moss is slippery
Veering to the left, veering to the right, stopping and
    going on again
Who goes with him? What does he lean on?
At the end of the road, the door of the hermitage
    opens to the east
Guest and host meet for a wordless talk
The mountain is silent, the streams sound like
    running water
The stone maiden argues and the wooden man scoffs
The blue-eyed barbarian came from the west in such
    a hurry
He leaked this message and buried the Buddha-sun
It was transmitted to an expert, workman Lu of Caoqi
He said that fundamentally there's not a single thing
How laughable [to see] everyone in the world ancient
    and modern
Using blows and shouts without [scruple of being false
    teachers], without sparing their eyebrows

Right now, what should I use to help contemporary
  people?
Spring, autumn, winter, summer are good seasons
If it's hot I go to the bank of a rushing stream, it it's
  cold I turn toward the fire
Cutting apart the white clouds that join at midnight
When tired I lie down at ease, nesting in the white
  clouds
The wind whistles in the pines
I invite you to come here to safeguard yourself for
  your remaining years
For hunger there are water plants, for thirst a spring

35. SONG OF CLOUDY MOUNTAIN

On the mountain white clouds are white
In the mountain flowing waters flow
This is where I want to live
The white clouds have opened up a place for me on
  the mountain
The white clouds say all there is to say about the
  things of the heart
Sometimes it rains and it's hard to stay long
Or I'm covered by the pure wind and it's easy
Traversing all the lands of the worlds of the galaxy
I will ride the pure wind along with you
Over rivers and mountains it drives us on everywhere
Drives us on—for what?
To be fit to play on the waves with the white gulls
I've come back to sit with the moon under the pines
The pines stir with a rustling sound
With whom can I talk of this Mind?
Countless buddhas and ancestral teachers are all
  talking freely
As I lie down lazily in the white clouds
The green mountain smiles at me completely
  unconcerned
I laugh and answer:
"Mountain, you don't know the reason I've come
My whole life I've never slept enough

I'd love these streams and rocks for my nightshirt"
So the green mountain laughed at me:
"Why didn't you come back to us earlier?
If you love the green mountains,
In the shadows of the trailing vines, cease and desist!"
I followed the green mountain's words
I abandoned my body and lay down on a spire of the
    green mountain
Sometimes I dream, sometimes I'm awake
Dreams and wakefulness do not hold me back
In dreams I turn back to seek the road on which I
    came
Riding a wooden ox in the wineshops of the capital
The wooden ox changes into the meaning of the
    spring wind
Flowers and willows in full bloom are like jade beads
Peach blossoms red as fire
Willow fuzz white as ermine
Within there's a plum blossom whiter than white
Wordlessness leads to a search in abstruse words
The cry of the wondrous animal [the "quarry" in the
    search for enlightenment] breaks the momentary
    dream
Still savoring the taste of sleep, the body does not stir

36. HOW TO STUDY ZEN

The days and months go by like lightning: we should value
the time. We pass from life to death in the time it takes to
breathe in and breathe out: it's hard to guarantee even a
morning and an evening. Whether walking, standing, sitting, or lying down, do not waste even a minute of time.
Become every braver and bolder. Be like our original
teacher Shakyamuni, who kept on progressing energetically.

    When the mind-ground is equanimous and awake and
still, you will have profound certainty in the intent of the
buddhas and ancestral teachers. You must accomplish this
correctly. Mind is the natural buddha: why bother seeking

elsewhere? Put down your myriad concerns and wake up. At the end of the road it's like an iron wall. False thoughts are all extinguished, and extinguishing is wiped away: body and mind seem to be resting on the void. In the stillness a light reaches everywhere with its brilliance.

The original face: who is it? As soon as it is mentioned, the arrow sinks in stone. When the mass of doubt is shattered amidst all the particulars, one thing covers the sky of blue. Do not talk of this with people without wisdom. Do not become overjoyed. You must visit Zen teachers: show them how your mind works and ask for their teaching. After that you can be called one who continues the tradition of the ancestral teachers.

Our family style is not remote. When tired we stretch out our legs and sleep. When hungry we let our mouths eat. In the human realm, what school is this? Blows and shouts fall like raindrops.

VERSES OF PRAISE

[Verses 37–103 were written upon giving Dharma names to people.]

37. "ANCIENT TRIPOD"

[Sobriquet of Elder Wen of Longquan]

The Other Side of the Primordial Buddha
Before the Empty Eon
One thing was there, hard as iron
Opening its great mouth, silent and speechless
Stepping across three incalculable ages, its journey
    has halted
Abandoning the whole body in a fiery pit
Savory food in the belly, incense filling the room
Mindlessly taking one step after another, cold and sad
Spilling one's guts to express the joy of Zen
Here the patchrobed monk is satisfied satisfied
    satisfied
Gautama's descendants still exist today

38. "HERMITAGE OF PROPER MEASURE"

[For an attendant at Mount Xiawu]

There is an elder of Mount Xiawu
Who goes through frost and snow unmindful of frost
    and snow
When the moon comes he allows its reflections
When the wind comes he lets the lonesome zither play
The sound of the lonesome zither is most Intimate
Listen well, don't let it leak away
From inside the reflections of the pure void, you must
    wipe them away
And comprehend that within it there is not a single
    thing
Let go: do not keep your knowledge
Why put gold dust in your eyes?
Do not stay with [the dichotomy of] knowing and not
    knowing
Only then will you meet the good season
You break Deshan's staff and shatter Linji's shout
Wherever you go you encounter people without being
    deceived by them
Only then can you pair the wind and the moon
With the wind but not the moon, there's no good light
With the moon but not the wind, there's no good talk
With a good wind and a good moon
Your Dharma play will never end

39. "IRON OX"

In the spring of *gui-mao* [1364] Chong Sodang visited me
on Mount Kaji. By the end of the summer retreat, I observed that his conduct was subtly refined, relaxed but
proper, and that he seemed to have the qualifications for
receiving the Path. Now in autumn he comes to say good-
bye, and asks for a sobriquet.

I am calling him "Iron Ox." The reason is this. Before
the end of the summer retreat, I asked the assembly about
their daily meditation work. Chong Sodang said: "In for-

mer days I understood in terms of the sound of Buddha and the form of Buddha. Since coming to this assembly, I have encountered the fundamental teaching. All my previous tricks are exhausted: I just coldly observe Zhaozhou's word *No*. I am like a mosquito on an iron ox."

So I have used his own words to give him a sobriquet. On this occasion I have composed a verse to present with it. Thus I lay on the whip hard and make the iron ox sweat, so he will meet Zhaozhou. Let him work hard on it.

So stupid and obstinate he doesn't look back
Without knowledge, how can he fear the lion's roar?
Not sleeping, but asleep, forever supine between
    heaven and earth
Neither going nor staying in the countless worlds of
    the galaxy
How many times the spring wind, how many times the
    fall!
The one body of suchness has no modern or ancient
When the fire at the end of the eon sweeps through,
    it does not burn This
The head and horns look the same in the fragrant
    grass and rain
Haven't you seen this ox plodding on so stupid and
    dull?
No one in the world can pull him along
Too bad the boy tending the ox has dropped the rope
He hasn't known what to do for a long time already
Today I urge the oxherd to advance
Let him step forward and jump up astride the ox and
    lash it to the marrow with the whip
The pain pierces to the marrow: out come sweat and
    blood
A colossal buddha-image comes to beg for help
I cannot help, I cannot do anything
Hanshan rubs his palms and laughs aloud
So you must visit a teacher of the school:
When your grasp is made certain
You will sing at leisure the Song of Great Peace

40. "WISDOM HERMITAGE"

[For Elder Song Gwangch'ong]

The eternal wind blows through the dark pines
The cool moon shines in the blue void
Without a fence, without a door
Deep blue vast and vacant, white bright and true
In between just space
The external objects are also Suchness
At this moment there's nowhere for the universal eye
    to search
In the heap of white clouds, a hut made of reeds
Fragrant grasses, falling flowers, spring sun and rain
The partridge call accompanies the tale of the
    bamboo flute
Where will the wanderer inquiring through the south
    go in the end?
Every atom of dust is this man's abode
Reduplications without end: the Flower Treasury
    World
The whole thing is right in this hermitage
The subtle wondrous truth in this
Fundamentally does not accommodate intellectual
    understanding
The host within the host is just like this
For long years he has never come out of the
    hermitage gate
He is totally free, without false contrivance, without
    selfish bias
He is utterly unconstrained, independent and
    sovereign
Even the slightest traces of views of ordinary and holy
    have been totally swept away
"Knowing" nothing, "understanding" nothing
Aaaah: what is it?
Though the season is cold, the pines in front of the
    hermitage do not change

41. "MOONLIGHT POND"

In the great expanse of silent sky
The round light shows alone
Its reflections go down to the depths of the pond
The light divides among the myriad waves spreading
out
The wondrous clear illumination
Can engulf the myriad images without omitting a
single one
The wondrous profound depths
Can contain the hundred streams without ever
overflowing
Light that penetrates a galaxy of worlds with
illumination to spare
It spreads in all directions like a great wave that never
overflows
The moon shines into the pond: they are not
different
The pond reflects the moon: they are not the same
Not different, not the same: this is Buddha
Aaaah—what words are these?
One moon is actually thirty days
Eternal night, pure sky
Wind in the pines cool and strong
This is the moonlight pond, a spirit land where there's
no "attainment"
It's not just the one color of an autumn midnight

42. TIME IS PRECIOUS

In the autumn of 1364 I happened to travel to Wollam
monastery. I composed this verse for the head of the
monks' hall there, Elder Yon of Kojo, to admonish him
about his daily activities.

By chance we meet in a season of purity
Together we recline among the blue-green mountains
and azure streams under the moon
Can we pass in vain this fair moment so hard to find?
In the jade-green gemstone the waters murmur

The murmuring waters in the jade-green gemstone
Impossible to buy even with a thousand pieces of gold
I invite you to empty your mind and listen to my
    words
Spring wind and autumn moon will not stop for your
    striped sideburns [your advancing age]

43. "WISDOM PEAK"

Knowledge cannot reach it, knowledge cannot fathom
    it
It props heaven and earth apart and produces being
    and emptiness
It stands alone on That Side beyond the last rays of
    illumination
Sudhana asks for another peak in vain
For ten thousand ages the flying white clouds have
    not been able to reach it
One morning the red sun peeps through and has
    already gotten there
However many times it has been through the fire at
    the end of an age, it is just like this
Lofty and awe inspiring down through the ages, it
    energizes the wind of the ancestral teachers

44. "HERMITAGE OF THE MEAN"

Zen man Shu-un from Japan has requested a verse to go
with his sobriquet. At present I am seventy-six years old:
my eyes are dim and I put aside the writing brush long
ago. His request was very earnest, so I forced myself to use
the old brush to say this:

In the thousand-layered jade-green mountains
On a dark green cliff ten thousand fathoms high
The delicate sound of the twisting mountain streams
    and flowing springs
Among the mixed trees of the deep forest it is empty
    but overgrown and lush

In the middle there's a little hermitage that seems not
    to be there
Morning and afternoon all that appears is the smoke
    of [the incense from] prayers to the Lord
Flowers fall, flowers bloom, birds do not come here
White clouds often come visiting at the gate
Does anyone know what the hermit does every day?
For long years he has not dreamed of the
    entanglements of the dusty sensory realm
Amidst the scene of quiet extinction [nirvana], he
    accompanies it, quiet and extinct
Green creepers up on the pines: pure wind and the
    moon

45. "THE OLD HERDSMAN"

Last year he sat on a hill tending an ox
Fragrant herbs by the side of the stream, drenching
    rain
This year he releases the ox and lies down on the hill
In the shade on a sunny day the warmth is less
He does not know whether to herd the old ox east or
    west
He puts down the rope and at leisure sings a song of
    no-birth
He turns back [to look]: the evening sun is red over
    the faraway mountains
Spring is ending: all over the mountain, falling
    flowers in the wind

46. "SNOWY PLUM EVES"

December snow fills the sky
On the cold plum tree the flowers are just opening
Snowflakes snowflakes snowflakes
As they scatter in among the plum blossoms, I really
    cannot tell them apart
Leaning on the fence all day long I cannot get enough
    of the view
Commission a painter to take up his brush and ink

Transfer a few branches to [a picture on] a screen
So that in the sweltering heat of August
It will refresh people's spirits

47. "SNOWY CLIFF"

In the snowy mountains, there's a snowy cliff
Above it there's white snow piled in peaks
Below, the first sprouts of grasses fragrant and green
It is called "fat grass"
Coming through three winters, it grows lush and
    thick, fair as jade
In the uniqueness of its color and flavor there is also
    sameness
In it there's the whiteness of a white ox, his fine hairs
    white as snow
The whiteness of the white ox is not white white
It's not that in white white there's another white
I urge you to mount this ox
Blow as you will on the one flute
There's a fragrance in the grass and flavor in the
    water
We wander satisfied in the snowy mountains
The joy in these mountains is not joy as you know it
We gladly share this joy with intimate acquaintances
I urge you not to pass your green spring wanderings
    in vain
You must intimately approach a teacher of the school
Constantly inquire of him, endure his tongs and
    hammer
The teacher will give you the fundamental provisions
Only after this will you be able to go or stay according
    to circumstances

48. "NO SPEECH"

Yon Sodang has given himself the sobriquet "No Speech."
Faithfully bearing a writing brush presented to him by the
king, he comes to seek a eulogy.

The dots and lines are like constellations
How can dragons and snakes be curved and bent?
Then there is dew from the sky
It descends to form droplets like pearls in the autumn
    moonlight
Bring them in and store them in the jade bowl
There is no time for precious jewels
The Zen teachers' Path is uncommon
Their talents are unique
Their reputation fills the world
Their words and deeds go together as one
Confucians and Buddhists respect their mystic wind
The dusts of sensory objects are ended: the fire has
    gone out in the ashes
They silently await those who come to learn
Peaceful and joyous and content
The intimate secret they have there with them
Cannot be communicated with words

49. "STUDIO OF CAREFUL CONDUCT"

What does it mean to be careful? Surely it refers to the
scrupulous sincerity in word and deed of the profound
person. He is careful with his words, so his words fill the
world without reproach. He is careful with his deeds, so
his deeds fill the world without regrets. Therefore, by being careful in word and deed, the superior person not only
has no worries or regrets; with every word and every act
he gives great constant norms to make the world and the
state endure forever.

Today Minister An Chinje has demanded some words
on the theme of his sobriquet "Studio of Careful Conduct."
T'aego has no choice but to give him a verse:

The realm, the state, in the old days and now—
This is the number-one jewel in managing the world
The orb of earth is bountiful everywhere
Heaven sends down a multitude of blessings

Every day unicorns of good omen appear in the
    courtyard
Every hour phoenixes of good order gather to fly and
    sing
Fragrant grasses, late spring rain
Cinnabar-red elms, November frost
With mind empty, observing the transformations of
    things
Having no concerns, just being ordinary

50. "HERMITAGE OF THE TRUE PATTERN"

Li, the true pattern, is the great norm for the realm and
the state. The sages use it to pacify everyone in the world.
The people are transformed by its virtue so that they all
return to their fundamental goodness. This pure wind
blows over the whole world: all the grasses bend down.

Today the state minister is seeking a sobriquet. I am
calling him Li An, "Hermitage of the True Pattern," and
I speak a verse to give witness. May the state minister perceive clearly what norms should be employed.

Knowledge cannot fathom it, knowledge cannot reach
    it
It embraces all of heaven and earth and runs through
    ancient and modern
It is naturally complete from before the beginning
There is no door on any side
Cliffs crumble, streams are cut off, the evening sun
    is red
Flowers fall, flowers open, so many mornings and
    evenings
The host within the host has never come or gone
Empty your mind and listen in silence to the sound
    of the wind in the pines
Don't try to ask the white clouds where they've
    traveled
This hermitage is basically at the end of the road of
    reason and "true patterns"

51. "THE FISHERMAN RECLUSE"

The master adepts of ancient times sometimes lived in seclusion as fishermen or woodcutters. They observed the wind and waited for the right time: then they would appear at court to utter a single word that would make the whole world return to correct customs and transform itself. [For the adepts such action in the world was as natural] as clouds following dragons and water flowing to the sea. How could anything not receive benefits from them? The great lords of Wei and Mei were such men.

The worthy minister Li An is also called "The Fisherman Recluse": this is where his intent lies. My verse for him says:

> The everlasting river is in the bright mirror
> It goes along with your lifelong purpose
> In the world there is nothing final
> Having cast with the fishing pole, put it down
> Ten thousand miles in a boat alone—one single moon
> Many notes from the eternal flute—the white gull
>   flies
> The august emperors of antiquity—where are they
>   now?
> Rising and falling for a thousand ages—only they
>   know
> Wait till the day the Yellow River is clear and shallow:
> Amidst wind and clouds, that will be the time of Great
>   Peace

52. "NOT REVEALED"

> A single spiritual illumination covers heaven and
>   earth
> Search inside and out—there's nowhere to get a grasp
> Thought ends, ideas are exhausted, you don't know
>   what to do
> Evidently you do not accept what [Buddha]
>   demonstrated by holding up the flower

Hurry up and study carefully: do not waste your days
in vain

53. "BAMBOO HERMITAGE"

Within it there's not a thing: it is fundamentally pure
No one in the whole world can get a glimpse inside
The phoenix cries, the dragon murmurs, breaking
the stillness of Zen
Atop a single pole the bright moonlight fills the river
city

54. "RETURNING TO THE SOURCE"

How many years have you drifted along the country's
rivers?
Today you turn your boat around and return to the
basic source
With a slight smile guest and host meet as they
intended
There's only this joy: no more descriptions or talk
Forms and words are cut off: there's no more
avoiding the taboo name
Utterly pure, clear and deep, no flavor at all

55. "THIS GATE"

The one road facing you points straight ahead
If you intentionally run to seek it, it's even more silent
and indistinct
Be thoroughly mindless, let everything go
Only then will you understand that the body of
thusness blocks nothing

56. "HERMITAGE OF THE PATH"

Perfectly peaceful, hard and solid, it cannot be
opened
In the masses of white clouds, it still looks the same
If today's people want to pass on the family business
They must go back to Vimalakirti's room

57. "IRON GATE"

So high you cannot climb up or get close to it
Raindrops scatter in the flying wind, the gate is
    barred with green moss
Suddenly forgetting thought, without attainment,
Only then will you be sure the gate has been open all
    along

58. "INNER TRUTH"

Moving or still within it according to the occasion
Benefiting the many beings equally, sharing in the
    myriad transformations
Letting go on That Side, beyond the thousand sages
This kind of great work perpetuates the family style

59. "SOURCE OF TRANSFORMATION"

Everything is totally real: fundamentally not one is
    there
Returning to the source there's no gain and no loss
The revered King of the Teaching of Great
Transcendent Wisdom
Is this Nirmanakaya Buddha right here now

60. "COMPLETE COMPREHENSION HERMITAGE"

With objects completely comprehended and persons
    emptied, even birds are scarce here
Falling flowers in the stillness, a patch of green moss
Unconcerned, the old monk faces the moon over the
    pines
And turns back to laugh at the clouds constantly
    coming and going

61. "SUCCESSORSHIP CLIFF"

Throughout the body is an iron heart
Eternal companion to the solitary pine and the moon
    in the cold

Giving birth to the spirit mushroom, spring sun and
  rain
In a mass of all kinds of flowers, leaning on a cloud

62. "REVELATION CLIFF"

Right where they are, form and matter are quiet and
  peaceful
After long silence in this inner state complete
  penetrating perception is difficult
The fire at the end of the age sweeps through and
  everything is gone
It's still the same as before amidst the white clouds

63. "NO SEVERITY"

The lion's roar, fearless teaching
Devas and demons fold their hands and all crumble
With blows and shouts scattering the spring wind
When red and white flowers open you know it's a
  good time

64. "CLOUD ROCK"

Among the floating clouds that cover it
It stands blunt and stupid, peaceful and still
How many times it has gone through good times of
  flowers in the moonlight
With mind long dead, I mindlessly look on

65. "STONE HERMITAGE"

Formed by nature hard
How could it fear wind and rain?
White clouds have been coming and going who knows
  how long
Unacquainted up till now with the host inside the
  hermitage

66. "HOW CAN I SPEAK?"

All phenomena are beyond names and forms
The sounds of the streams and the colors of the
    mountains are closest
What is "closest"?
You can only please yourself: how can I speak?

67. "THIS PATH"

At the assembly on Spirit Peak it was personally
    entrusted
Today as before we face the reed hut
If you use conceptual mind to try to figure it out
You are afflicting your mind even more with deceitful
    cleverness

68. "PASSING THROUGH THE CLOUDS"

My whole life my going and staying have had no
    starting point
Where there is no seeking, there is peace
I have traveled all over the world without leaving a
    trace
Today as before I lie down among the jade-green
    mountains

69. "MERGING WITH THE VOID"

Empty but aware, void but wonder-working
Without "knowledge," illumination is complete
Though among the myriad phenomena, not standing
    in relative opposition to them
Responding to their potentials by manifesting an
    ocean of meditative states beyond measure

70. "CUT-OFF HERMITAGE"

The road on the other side of the green mountain is
    cut off from worldly entanglements
Nor do any buddhas or Zen masters come to its gate

The hundred birds with flowers in their beaks have
    stopped going and coming
Just the smoke of a candle dedicated to the
Enlightened Lord

71. "WITHOUT FEAR"

The fire at the end of the age will not burn This
The place where Buddha is born is immovable
Blank and unconcerned I face the green mountain
My eyes are higher than the world: devas and demons
    salute

72. "HIDDEN PEAK"

A billion Sumerus are within it
Thousands of layers of white clouds surround it
The last rays of illumination from That Side are weak
    and dim outside
But it stands majestically, energizing the ancient wind

73. "WHERE TO STAY"

I don't stay on this side or That Side
Nor is the Middle Path my abode
Letting the rivers and mountains roll out and roll up
I smile at the white gull at ease on the waves

74. "NO KNOWLEDGE"

Sitting alone, always like a stupid oaf
The dead trees on the cold cliff encounter green
    spring
Red dust, purple fields, no more rushing around
Hiding this body all along in the cloudy mountains

75. "CLOUDY MOUNTAINS"

White clouds—inside the clouds, layers of green
    mountains

Green mountains—in the mountains, many white
  clouds
The sun is the constant companion of the cloudy
  mountains
When the body is at peace, there's no place that's not
  home

76. "HELPLESS"

With mind and objects both forgotten—what is it?
Are the white flowers and the color of the snow one
  or not?
The road to That Side is subtle and hard to reach the
  end of
Traversing all the thousand rivers, the moon with no
  reflections

77. "THE PEAK OF SUBTLE WONDER"

The subtle wonder of the jagged peaks: form is not
  form
The visage beyond the peaks: silent infinity
Its beautiful light shines from above on the world
No one on earth can find it

78. "NO ATTACHMENTS"

Going on this way, fundamentally without seeking
Going on otherwise, also independent
East, west, south, north, the road of perfect
  penetration
Every day exultant, free to go or stay

79. "NO PATTERN"

One thing that exhausts form and sound
Formless and nameless
The myriad forms of being arise from this
Material transformations seem like spirit work

80. "NO REALIZATION"

Final realization is still a reflection of the light
Complete enlightenment is still a little vague
Sweep away the dark abstruse mystic wonder
It's pure and cool all the way to the bone

81. "EMPTY STREAM"

The tracks of millions of people are cut off
The traveler over three immeasurable eons reaches
    the end of the road
The fallen flowers float on the jade-green pure
    stream
The white sun penetrates west and east

82. "STONE STREAM"

One flows, one doesn't flow
There is silence and its opposite
Where do the cries and murmurs return?
I remember the one color of the eternal sky

83. "THE MIDDLE SEA"

The ten directions come from this station
The myriad phenomena meet in this source
Ten billion layers of watery abyss
Can be hidden in a mustard seed

84. "OCEAN CLOUDS"

Over the vast and boundless blue-green ocean
White clouds travel one after another
The white gulls take joy in their midst
I'll allow you this life

85. "CLOUDY RAVINE"

The clouds are companions to the white sun
The waters are neighbors to the pure sky

Inexhaustible bliss beyond the world
Who will share in the joy?

86. "THE PATH OF EMPTINESS"

This emptiness is not empty emptiness
This Path is not a path that can be considered a path
Where peaceful extinction is totally extinct
Perfect illumination is complete and final

87. "ONE GATE"

The whole world is one gate:
Why don't you come in?
When you have penetrated Zhaozhou's *No,*
At last the chains will open by themselves

88. "ONE STREAM"

The stream that runs through the thousand ages
Washes away all the shadows of the two sides
How laughable Lord Huang of Jin
He sought again and again without comprehending

89. "INDETERMINATE"

It stays on neither side
It cuts off causes and conditions past, present, and
    future
If you believe in this thing
What's within you covers heaven and earth

90. "HERMITAGE OF REALIZATION"

No wall in any direction
No gate on any side
Buddhas and patriarchs do not get here
Sleeping at ease among the white clouds

91. "STONY CREEK"

The sound of the rolling rocks murmurs
The long and broad tongue [of Buddha] without bias
Though it teaches all equally
It does not explain for those unable to hear

92. "EMPTY VALLEY"

Vast and broad, it covers heaven and earth
Close and intimate, it contains the pure void
Buddhas and enlightened teachers cannot find it
But they can build reed huts

93. "A STRETCH OF OCEAN"

On the vast flooding waves
A boat, and the flute's eternal note
Once you've heard it, sentiments and sense objects are
    smashed
The white gull dances upward in flight

94. "THIS VALLEY STREAM"

It does not flow—the moon of this side
Flowing by That Side—the clouds
A thousand ages are hidden in the deep blue
The falling flowers extend in profusion

95. "FRIENDS MOUNTAIN"

The mountain directly points out the road for the
    returning traveler
Its benevolence is higher than the Peak of Lofty
    Wonder
Even having one's body shattered is not sufficient
    recompense
Modern and ancient, there are no tracks for climbing
    it

96. "WONDROUS PEAK"

Its awesome heights overarch the cosmos
Its lofty level summit pierces the heavens
Mountains far and near all look up in admiration
Clouds moving back and forth float by on their own

97. "THE PURE STREAM"

It issues from the green mountain valley
Flowing on to the blue-green sea
The sound of the rushing water is most intimate
Does anyone know how to approach and listen?

98. "THE INNER MOON"

It does not dwell in east or west
Hundred percent pure light permeates everything
Revealed alone within the myriad forms
Perfect illumination eternal and indestructible

99. "NOT JEWELS"

Though gold and jade fill the hall
Actually these are not the precious things that will
    save us
Follow this jewel of mine birth after birth:
Study Zen with unified mindfulness of the Real

100. "THE ANCIENT FOREST"

Trees with no branches or leaves
The spring wind stirs their roots
They are not white or green in color
The flowers open without a trace

101. "A TIME OF PEACE"

One stroke pacifies all under heaven
Myriad nations come to offer congratulations

Success in Korea is won up on the ramparts
The children sing lee-la

102. "LOYAL AND SCRUPULOUS"

Your pure discipline is the best in Korea
Your accomplishments and fame will last ten
    thousand generations
You always honor and serve the Lord
Even when busiest, your mind does not change

103. "HERMITAGE OF BLISS"

In the mountains, a hut of reeds
In a dream, a stipend of a thousand silver ingots
Recite the buddha-name to achieve success
It's the land of ultimate bliss in this life

104. "NO ABILITY"

This matter is fundamentally unborn
Following circumstances, it is clear everywhere
With certain comprehension of this message
You return home and can stop asking the way there

105. A VERSE FOR A DISCIPLE

The Zen of patchrobed monks is one hundred
    percent clear
The pines of the age-old forest are in the courtyard
How ridiculous for the son of the City of Blessing
To travel south to search through a hundred other
    towns

106. TO A CHINESE ZEN MAN IN JAPAN

Thus do I communicate, thus do you comprehend. For
me there is truly no gain and loss. For you, master, how
could there be no merit? In the eastern sea, a mountain
range stands out: Japan, a spot of red. Too bad the disciple
standing in the snow almost lost the family style.

107. ONE TUNE

[To Master Wuji, a man of Jiangnan]

Coming from the West, one tune, with no one to
    recognize it
Though there was a master musician, there was no
    worthy disciple to harmonize
Sitting alone in the desolate emptiness deep into the
    night
Penetrating through the shade, the last rays of
    moonlight suffuse the Zen robe

108. HOW LONG?

The green springtime [of youth], then we add white
    hair
The white sun of noon deceives us about the red [to
    come at sunset]
So let me ask you about the floating things [of the
    world]:
How long can they be at peace?

109. FOLLOW THEIR EXAMPLE

[Two verses in answer to Kim Hui-jo]

The pure body of the Tathagata
In former days was a person caught in revolving
    rebirth
Confucius too was once among the rabble and in
    the soldiers' ranks
How can we follow their example?
Nothing is as good as seeking the reality of mind
Be careful not to seek from others
Or you will bury away and lose your own family jewels

Always going in and out through the six gates [of the
    senses]
From the beginning it has always been the boss
If you act in vain as a traveler on the road
You will meet the eight winds [of evil influences] all
    the time

Better to study this business:
Come travel in the snowy mountains
And inquire where it has gone
Only thus will you comprehend this thing perfectly

110. THIS FLOWER

[Answer to Yom Hung-bang]

It's not spring, but in this place this flower blooms
It lets the floating clouds come and go in the void
Where it stands is Thus, and Thusness does not
    change
Why must we add a jewel canopy to the royal
    carriage?

111. ENTER THE FAMILY OF THE BUDDHAS

[Answer to Yi Pang-jik]

Sensory afflictions and what you think you know are
    both barriers
Totally forget knowledge and understanding, do not
    follow others
Let us go on like two fools who have forever cut off
    even the least little thing
Complete realization with nothing left out: we enter
    the family of the buddhas

112. SEEING OFF AN INDIAN MONK

From India, a true son of Buddha
His bodily existence as free as the white clouds
I entrust these words to the mountains and the waters
You must open your barbarian blue eyes and look

113. SEEING OFF A JAPANESE MONK

East of the ocean, the moon of a thousand ages
Over Jiangnan, ten thousand miles of sky
The Pure Light has not this or that
Do not accept parochial Zen

114. THIS FAIR TIME

[Seeing off the two Zen masters Yong and Koeng]

Haven't you read of Siddhartha's travels in the
    blue green mountains?
He warned you that in the time it takes to breathe in
    and out, you may relinquish human life
He urged you to use your profound mind to come to
    grips with sayings of subtle wonder
This fair time is hard to come by: how can we waste it?
In countless ages to come, there won't be a time like
    this
The will of people of greatness is precisely like this

115. DO NOT SPURN LIVING BEINGS

[Seeing off Zen man Hye]

Traveling over rivers and seas without moving a foot
As you cross mountains and streams, do not go in vain
The legitimate business of patchrobed monks
Is to seek teachers and inquire after the Path, without
    spurning living beings
If you do not spurn living beings
You will soon meet an enlightened teacher with the
    mastery to sort you out decisively
You will smash the gloom of ignorance
And cut off the tongues of everyone in the world
Only then will your heart be at peace
When you come back to my gate here
There will be nothing to stop you demonstrating your
    transcendent perfection

116. T'AEGO'S FAREWELL TO MASTER SHIWU

The disciple T'aego Po-u had long heard of Shiwu's [repu-
tation for attainment in the] Path. Not considering a thousand miles too far [to come], he paid a visit to the peak of
Mount Xiawu and did indeed study with Shiwu in his private room. It was like the prodigal son meeting his father.

    T'aego stayed with Shiwu a fortnight, getting decisive

instruction on the essentials of Mind and getting his fill of the milk of the Dharma. Shiwu's benevolence was so great that it would be hard to repay even by having one's body pulverized.

Now it comes time to say farewell. How could there be no feelings? I now eulogize Shiwu's virtue and proclaim my vows. Composing a verse, I present it to him, to show my sincerity.

> We observe the teacher's great perfect mirror
> We also observe the disciple's everywhere equal
>   nature
> Together they are a single body that extends
>   throughout space
> Empty and open, the light pervades everything,
>   without a shadow
> No living beings, no buddhas, no subject or object
> Luminous awareness reaches everywhere, clear and
>   pure and always still and shining
> The dense array of myriad images appears within it
> Our teacher shows the shape of the moon in the water
> The disciple's body is also there like a flower in the
>   water
> Clean and dirty, suffering and bliss, all appear
> Now a certain disciple within our teacher's great
>   perfect mirror
> Takes refuge with and pays homage to our teacher,
>   an ancient buddha in the disciple's mirror
> He sincerely vows to specially protect [the teacher's
>   legacy]
> To be like this lifetime after lifetime, birth after birth
> The teacher is the master of the Flower Treasury
>   World
> I act as his eldest son to assist in his beneficent work
> When he lived in Tushita Heaven exounding the
>   Dharma there
> I was a deva chief always standing by to protect him
> When we sat beneath the bodhi tree
> I was a king acting as a patron to the Dharma

According to my fundamental vow today
All kinds of adornments have been perfectly
    prepared
I offer them to the infinite numbers of buddhas of
    the ten directions
The Great Vehicle bodhisattvas and everyone else,
Along with all the children of the buddhas in the
    whole universe,
Together witness the inner truth of the tathagatas,
    eternal and still
They obliterate all afflictions and defilements till
    none remain
They achieve all the wondrous practices
Through all the buddha-assemblies of the future
They must meet each other as guests and host in turn
The teacher as the central pole, me as the satellite
The teacher as the satellite, me as the central pole
We go on for all time to come doing the buddha-work
Delivering all sentient beings, then after we return,
Wandering together in supreme great nirvana
All the same as today's excursion on Mount Xiawu
Though in illusory substance we are separated into
    this and that
This Mind never leaves our side

117. FAREWELL TO THE ROYAL TEACHER

What should those who leave home [to become Buddhist monks] do? Forever cut off the duties of worldly entanglements.

Today I bid farewell to the Royal Teacher, and he asks where I am going. I am originally a man of the mountains, and I must go dwell in the mountains. I do not long for walks in the blue-green mountains, I do not shun running around in the red dusts [of the human world]. I do this to suit the feelings of my own true nature, and to cultivate virtue so that I can repay our enlightened lord.

When we look at them [realistically], worldly glory and infamy are like aggregations of bubbles. If I stayed here too long, my repute would lead [people into] many errors. Better to forget [people's ideas of] right and wrong, and hide among the birds and beasts in the forest ravines. The forest streams have a mystic flavor.

If the Sage Lord will extend his protection to me, he will grant me the favor of letting me go off to spend my old age in the green mountains. What is there in the mountains? Blue sky and mist. Thus would I cultivate the work of the Path, send down the rain of the Dharma on the nation, and devote myself to praying for the long life of our Sage Ruler, burning incense morning and night.

118. VERSES ON SHAKYAMUNI BUDDHA

SHAKYAMUNI DWELLING IN THE MOUNTAINS

Praise?—you have no virtues
Blame?—you have no faults
Forgetting your wife and son and parents was very
    unfilial
Six years you sat cold and starving

SHAKYAMUNI LEAVING THE MOUNTAINS

People say it's Shakyamuni
They also call him Siddhartha
Don't! Don't! Stop talking of dreams!
He is not an optical illusion
Grand and free, naked and unfettered
Peaceful and far reaching, pure and bare
The spring wind spreading light over the free waters
Walking alone through heaven and earth—who will
    accompany me?
If I encountered a faithful disciple on the mountain
How could I send him down from the mountain with
    yellow leaves [instead of true gold]?
His virtue so lofty and unsurpassable no praise is
    adequate
His mercy so deep and measureless it's beyond
    reproach

For countless ages, scrupulously cultivating practices
    of subtle wonder
Incalculable as the sands of the Ganges
Now he leaves home to go into the snowy mountains
Cries of sorrow from parents and wife break his heart
They break his heart—pain pierces to the bone
How would they know his true compassion will save
    the world?
Stop! Stop! Don't be stupid!
It is not a dream, so don't call it a dream
It seems like a dream, but it's not a dream
It's just this Shakyamuni Buddha
Quiescent and inactive and forever unmoving
Naked and free and unbound
True comprehension that's impossible to grasp
What is the voice of the living Shakyamuni?
Under the evening sun the gulls spontaneously call
    out his name

119. MANJUSRI

He holds up the sword [of transcendent wisdom] so
    sharp it cuts a hair blown across it
His family style is wondrous, unique
Moving free beyond the thousand sages
The moonlight shines on the white flowers in the
    snow

120. GUANYIN

The color of her empty body of illusory
    transformation is ever fresher
You may set eyes on her, but she doesn't allow
    intimacy
After the spring wind on the riverbank of golden sand
The scattering mess [of fallen blossoms] is deep red,
    saddening everyone to death
Saddening people to death so they won't be deceived
If gap-toothed Bodhidharma came again, who would
    want to see him?

Alas! Who would not recognize your many kinds of
ugliness?

121. BODHIDHARMA

Breaking apart empty space
Coming forth majestic and alone
Cutting off everything on top of Vairocana's head
Neither Buddha nor Dharma before his eyes
No Buddha, no Dharma: heaven is high and earth is
    flat
Not mind, not things: rivers are green and mountains
    are blue
So he brought this tune across the ocean
In front of the king of Liang he snapped his fingers
One snap and one snap more
The hidden valleys change color and the flowing
    springs resound
I urge you to listen—have no other thoughts
I'm afraid bystanders will deliberately join in to get
    to hear
Those who are [superficially] acquainted with him fill
    the world
But how many know his mind?

Bodhidharma came from the west, sailing thousands
    of miles across the sea
Just to transmit the One Matter [of enlightenment]
He was face to face with the king of Liang, but their
    tunes were not the same
He was like the full moon of autumn in an empty sky
When he crossed the Great River to Wei on a single
    reed
The pure wind escorted him and leveled the waves
Too bad the old man fishing on the riverbank
Did not push him over the moment he saw him
If he had pushed him over, there would have been
    no coming or going
Avoiding the pain later of [his successor] Shen-guang
    cutting off his arm

Thousands of miles he came: to do what?
Each and every person has a pair of eyebrows
Carrying just one shoe, he went back west
In vain he makes his descendants talk about right and
    wrong
Wrong is not wrong, right is not right
The yellow chrysanthemum of the double-yang
    autumn festival leans on the eastern hedge
Before you had come, the world was at peace
When you had gone back, the seas and rivers were
    clear
The white clouds on Bear Ear Mountain could not
    hide you
For a thousand ages, they have transmitted your
    empty name

As you sat coldly for nine years silent and speechless
No matter how many doubted you, they could not do
    anything about you
To a man standing in the snow [Shen-guang, the
    second patriarch of Zen in China] you passed on
    the intimate message
With the spring wind, flowers opened everywhere
Before the blue-eyed teacher [Bodhidharma] came
Everyone's nostrils were dragging through the sky
When he returned to the west carrying one shoe
Everyone had a complete set of eyebrows and eyes
Why did he come and go like this?
If we look at it coldly, it's a cause for laughter

Spirit head, demon face
Bushy eyebrows, gap teeth
Sitting alone at Shaolin, holding in the poison breath
Returning to the west with one shoe, truly alive

For the true true meaning of [Bodhidharma's]
    coming from the west
It's best to be silent and relate nothing
What are you angry at?
Buddha is the dust before your eyes

122. BUDAI

Neither monk nor layman, a man of great leisure
Over blue mountains and purple fields, a life of
    independence
Sometimes he cavorts in wineshops
Spring wind fills his face, he forgets natural reality
A red face after a sad parting
Only with white hair will they get close again

123. THE BODHISATTVA MEDICINE KING

Medicine King! Medicine King!
You open the door of great compassion
You do not forget your earlier vow to save sentient
    beings
If you don't save us from the suffering of illnesses
    caused by karma,
How could this be called a bodhisattva's practice of
    great compassion?

124. THE SIXTH PATRIARCH

[Huineng of Caoqi, "Workman Lu"]

As he happened to hear the *Diamond Sutra*
It switched his eyes around
Because he venerated the Dharma
He did not fear the journey
When he visited Huang Mei, the fifth patriarch was
    getting old
Peach blossoms red, plum blossoms white, willows so
    green
We can sympathize with all the days he spent on the
    treadmill wearing a weight
But for him, how could there be the least bit of
    trouble?
[For him] the grain had already been ripe a long time
In the middle of the night, he entered the fifth
    patriarch's room

The fifth patriarch personally passed on to him the
    Dharma robe
[Due to the jealousy of other followers of the fifth
    patriarch] his life was hanging by a thread
So he secretly crossed the West River by moonlight
Who knew at that time?—he was glad to leave

125. SELF-PRAISE

[At the request of Chang Hae]

An East Asian body with Indian bones
An eye in my belly black as lacquer
So I wrapped an arrow in tangled artemisia
And traveled across the world without expressing my
    meaning
Suddenly I bumped into the old man on Mount
    Xiawu
The more I held it back, the more I revealed the
    totally deadly poison
I have not peddled this bit of energy east and west
I came back to my old mountain
I don't argue right and wrong with worldly people
Through long years without concerns I listen to the
    wind in the pines

126. A TALK AT YONGNING ZEN TEMPLE

[A talk requested by his disciples the day T'aego opened the
teaching hall at Yongning Zen Temple in (modern Beijing),
the capital of the Yuan dynasty.]

This realm has given birth to me, just as in a mustard
seed are hidden ten billion lands. Bah!

How crude and coarse this village monk is! Accepting
the imperial will, I wrongly expose the ugliness of my family. Rebuking the buddhas and ancestral teachers, I therefore create karmic suffering. Ha ha ha.

From now on I won't act like this. I will go straight into
the mountains and live with the monkeys and tigers.

127. AFTERWORD TO THE *PURE RULES OF BAIZHANG*

[From an edition printed by order of Emperor Xuan Ling]

The subtle wonder handed down from buddha to buddha and from enlightened teacher to enlightened teacher is not a matter of predetermined guidelines. Nevertheless, if people have no standards of behavior, they will be unable to adjust the workings of their minds properly. Therefore, all the sages since high antiquity have both practiced [proper standards] and imparted lessons [about them] unendingly.

Nowadays our Sage Lord honors and believes in these [pure rules] and has by his command caused them to be put into circulation [throughout the realm]. This must be because he planted [the seeds of] the light of prajna in past lives and had practiced the practices of the great vows of the universally good one, Samantabhadra. Can all of us who encounter His Majesty's sagely transformative influence do other than rejoice and cultivate these pure rules?

128. PREFACE TO
ADMONITORY LESSONS FOR THE MONASTIC COMMUNITY

Of all the people in the whole world, who does not have buddha-nature? Who does not have the mind of faith? Nevertheless, if people do not encounter the teachings of the sages, they do not unfurl the mind of supreme enlightenment, and they sink forever in the sea of sufferings, appearing and disappearing, going on and on in vain through birth and death. This is really to be pitied!

Therefore, the buddhas and enlightened teachers and sages have acted as uninvited friends and practiced uncaused compassion, and explained all kinds of expedient methods for people. They have taught and transformed and tamed people, to enable them to give rise to the pure mind of faith, and achieve the supreme fruit of buddhahood, enlightenment.

Enlightenment, the supreme fruit of buddhahood:

could it be anything else? It is each and every person's fundamental enlightened mind. The *Great* [*Perfection of Wisdom*] *Sutra* also says so: "If you want to know the Tathagata's great nirvana, you must completely understand your own fundamental nature." If people profoundly believe in these words, suddenly they will look back and recognize the infinite wondrous truths within inherent mind, fundamentally complete of itself with the hundreds of thousands of samadhis. Not a bit of it is false. This is the mind of correct faith. When the sages of past, present, and future appear in the world, and create words in the midst of wordlessness, it is precisely to talk about this.

When I journeyed south [in China] in search of the Dharma, I was lucky enough to encounter these *Admonitory Lessons*. Having returned to my native land Korea, I have wanted for years to have this book circulated widely here, to benefit the nation and the people. Now we have the outstanding man Ming Hue, who has vowed to arrange for the printing and distribution. This will enable the people of our country, once they read this or hear it read, to create an excellent causal basis so that they may finally achieve supreme correct enlightenment together [with all the enlightened ones]. This is the great meaning of the *Admonitory Lessons*.

129. LETTER FROM MASTER SHIWU TO T'AEGO

As I recall, in the seventh month, Elder T'aego, not shrinking from the perils of the long journey, came to my mountain peak, seeking definitive resolution of his own [great] matter [of enlightenment]. At the time we met, for me, there was no dharma that could be talked about, and for him, there was no word to be heard. This was a true meeting. If there is the least pretext that allows for talk, fundamentally, all of these are the thorns of opinions. This is the true pattern of the meetings of all the ancients.

Elder T'aego, while preserving and nurturing himself, showed more and more [of his realization], and avoided following perverted views. Elder T'aego came to this mountain on the seventeenth day of the twelfth month. I am glad to hear that he has returned [safely] to the great capital, but I do not know whether he will stay there or return home, so I have cut this short. Above all I hope he will take the great Dharma as the most important thing. This is what I pray for.

Last month, twenty-ninth day, Zhi Zheng era, *ding-hai* year [1348]. A letter to Elder T'aego Po-u from the old monk Qinghong of Shiwu who dwells on Mount Xiawu in Huzhou.

130. LETTER FROM T'AEGO TO MASTER SHIWU

Your disciple Po-u of Chunghung Zen Temple in Korea bows nine times and responds:

Since the first day of the eighth month when I left you, Master Shiwu, on Xiawu Mountain, not a day goes by that I don't think of you. Journeying over good roads, I arrived back at the capital on the fifteenth day of the tenth month. The awl in the bag showed through a bit: the virtuous ones of the Zen establishment and the great ministers of the imperial court reported to the emperor, and by his will I now serve as abbot of Yongning Zen Temple. The crown prince presented me with a golden monk's robe, and a whisk fragrant as incense.

Heaven's command had brought together Buddhist laity and clergy from all over. Hundreds and thousands and tens of thousands gathered around at the beat of the drum. I had no choice but to ascend to the teacher's seat: I saluted [the emperor] and lit the incense of good fortune. Then I took out a stick of incense from inside my robe for you, Old Teacher, and gave an account of the vehicle of the Zen school and held up the Teaching for the Last Age of the Dharma. But how could this repay your great benevolence [in feeding me] the milk of the Dharma? I dare not fail to report, it was a scene of the family's ugliness, a mess of low slang, trying hard to describe [reality to people].

I hope to join you again next spring: till the end of my life I will always faithfully serve you. If I am held back by karmic entanglements and I do not in fact get to return home to you, I will always go by what you taught me: benefiting self and others according to what's appropriate, and not selling the Buddha Dharma cheap, so that we do not cut off our posterity in the future. Nevertheless, this is scarcely something I can do on my own: the basic vow of all buddhas and Zen adepts supports and upholds this.

A while ago I visited you and thereby succeeded to the Great Work. Today in obedience to an imperial order I open a teaching hall: this too has its compelling cause. How could I dare with my clumsy words to try to set forth in full all my crude feelings? I humbly hope I can follow your example scrupulously, and visit you again and again.

I hope that myriad blessings will come to you, Master, my Fundamental Teacher, in all that you do, and that the people in your home area will benefit as your compassion extends among them and you bring them peace of mind.

131. MASTER SHIWU'S REPLY TO T'AEGO

After you went back, my old sickness got more serious by the day, so I shut my gate and took care of myself, prolonging my time for a little longer. On the thirteenth day of the tenth month of *wu-zi* [1348] a messenger from Jing Ci Temple unexpectedly delivered your letter. As I read it I realized that for T'aego time and circumstances are both ripe. The experienced worthies of the Zen temples and the great ministers and high officials have informed the emperor about you, and you are now abbot of Yongning Zen Garden. Opening a hall and expounding the Dharma, you are showing the teachings of our school. This is because your inner state is genuine and in accord with sagehood, so that the real substance of what you do moves people. How could this be so by chance?

You also let me know that on the day you opened the teaching hall, you held up a stick of incense for me, old and inept as I am. [I was touched, but], when I went away and had some free time and I had stopped my crazy false thoughts, how could I falsely think myself to be anyone's teacher? That you are like this now must be due to circumstances meshing over many births.

So when you appear in the world to help people, you must use the fundamental matter to stimulate and lead the immature ones who come to learn. Be careful not to use the devices and perspectives [of Zen] to flatter and play up to others. If everybody rolls around in the weeds, what can we hope to accomplish? You must work hard on it yourself. If you can actually be this way, you will not deviate from beginning to end. Then at the same time you repay in full the benevolence of the emperor and the benevolence of the Buddha.

What more shall I say? Though the road between us is far, thousands of miles, we still have each other in view. Old and tired, I cannot reply fully enough: please forgive me.

Eighth year of *Zhi Zheng* [1348], eleventh month, seventh day. Shiwu of Mount Xiawu sends salutations.

GLOSSARY

AMITABHA   *See* Buddha.

ANANDA   Disciple and constant attendant of Shakyamuni Buddha, with faithful recall of his verbal teachings; reckoned as the second patriarch of Zen in India.

BIRTH AND DEATH   *Samsara,* the opposite of nirvana: the life-cycle of sentient beings in their ordinary state of ignorance, marked by conditioned perception, false sense of self vs. others, impermanence, suffering, lack of stable identity; in the elementary forms of Buddhism the goal is first presented as escape from samsara.

BODHI   Enlightenment, direct awareness of reality, complete comprehension of worldly and transcendent truth; wisdom and compassion are inherent in bodhi.

BODHIDHARMA   An Indian monk ca. 500 c.e., named in Zen lore as the twenty-eighth patriarch of Zen in India and the first patriarch of Zen in China; he visited the emperor of South China, a devout patron of Buddhism, who did not understand him, then went north to dwell in seclusion at Shaolin Temple, awaiting a worthy successor. Called familiarly "the barbarian monk," "the red-bearded barbarian," "the blue-eyed barbarian."

BODHISATTVA   An enlightening being, one who enables others to develop enlightened perception. To function as a bodhisattva is the aim of Great Vehicle Buddhism as a whole, and of Zen. See Thomas Cleary (trans.), *The Flower Ornament Scripture,* 3 vols. (Shambhala Publications, 1984–1987).

BUDDHA   An enlightened one. According to Great Vehicle Buddhism, all sentient beings are potentially enlight-

169

ened: their real nature is to be buddhas. Hence there are many buddhas, past, present, and future. Famous figures in the Buddhist teachings include:

AMITABHA BUDDHA: The buddha of infinite life, the buddha of infinite light, located in the West, in a paradise called the Land of Bliss; through faith in Amitabha and by invoking his name, Pure Land Buddhists hope to be reborn with Amitabha in the western paradise, where their quest for enlightenment can proceed unhindered by the troubles of our world of suffering.

SHAKYAMUNI BUDDHA (also called Gautama, and Siddhartha):   The buddha of the present era, the historical buddha, the founder of Buddhism; a prince of the Shakya clan, who left home, achieved enlightenment after strenuous efforts, and set the Wheel of the Teaching turning in classical India in the fifth century B.C.E.

MAITREYA BUDDHA   The future buddha, the merciful buddha, destined to come down to be born on earth and to preside over a new era of social justice, peace, and prosperity; a focus of millenarian expectations in East Asian popular Buddhism.

VAIROCANA BUDDHA   The universal illuminator, the buddha representing the absolute reality pervading all particulars in all worlds; the center of the mandala; the solar buddha.

BUDDHA BODIES   Buddha is said to have three bodies:

dharmakaya, "the body of reality," the ground of all being, indescribable, inconceivable, beyond dualities, present in everything; all the buddhas share one and the same dharmakaya.

nirmanakaya, "the form body," "the body of magical transformation," the diverse physical forms which buddha takes on to communicate with sentient beings in diverse worlds.

sambhogakaya, "the body of bliss," "the reward body," buddha as experienced by bodhisattvas, for whom action in the world and transcendent realization are seamlessly fused.

BUDDHA-NATURE   Our true identity, which is to be buddhas.

CAOQI   *See* Huineng.

CLOUDS   Symbolic of illusory experience; the white clouds of illusion obscure the green mountain of reality.

DAO (old spelling: Tao)   "The Path," "the Way"; in classical Chinese philosophy, the term for the inherent pattern of reality, which furnishes the proper moral orientation for self and society; used in Buddhist parlance as a synonym for the path of enlightenment.

DESHAN (781–867)   A classic Zen master; noted for teaching with blows of his staff. He said, "Our school has no words; in reality there is no doctrine to be given to people."

DEVAS   The celestial beings of Indian cosmology: "the gods" who in Buddhist imagery come to offer praises and shower down heavenly flowers to salute the enlightened.

DHARMA   All phenomena are dharmas: things, events, perceptions, concepts, teachings. *The* Dharma, the Buddha Dharma, is the reality taught by the enlightened ones; in this sense *Dharma* means "truth" or "the true teaching" or "true reality." Buddhism teaches that true reality pervades and is present within all particular phenomena: that all dharmas are Dharma.

DHARMAKAYA   *See* buddha bodies.

EMPTINESS   *Sunyata,* the identityless nature of all phenomena; all phenomena are the result of an interplay of conditioning causal factors, and have no independent, stable identity beyond that; moreover, the temporary characteristics of phenomena as perceived are as they are only relative to the mentality of the perceivers.

EMPTY EON   In classical Indian cosmology, every world system moves from an age of emptiness on through ages of creation, abiding, destruction, and then another "empty eon" of nothingness between cycles; "before the Empty Eon" in Zen means before this universe came to be, at the level of Mind.

EXPEDIENT MEANS   The teaching of the Buddha Dharma is adjusted to the mentality of those to whom the teaching is being addressed; different truths pertain to learners at different levels; all particular formulations of the Dharma are just provisional expedients to communicate the Dharma in specific contexts; Buddhist teachings are not dogmatic doctrines, but skillful means: devices and strategies and methods to lead minds to reality.

EYE   The eye of enlightenment, the "eye on the forehead," the eye that both sees absolute reality and discerns truly among differentiated worldly phenomena.

THE FORMER KINGS   The Confucian paragons of just and creative rulership, for example Yao and Shun; the Sage Kings of antiquity who ruled in accord with the Path and its power, accomplishing great political feats by moral force, whose civilizing policies were selfless and suited to the needs of the times.

FOX   "The wild fox," skittish, clever, wary, is a symbol of the rationalizing faculty of the human mind that tries to conceptualize wisdom and thereby obscures it.

GAUTAMA   *See* Buddha.

GOLDEN RAVEN   Symbol of the sun, of *yang; see* Yin-Yang.

GREAT PEACE   *Taiping,* the classical Chinese term for utopia, a society based on the Dao, where there is free circulation of material goods and mutual respect, whose different layers enjoy harmony and free intercommunication. In Buddhism, it is used as a symbol of the richness of experience and creative action of the enlightened person returning to the world.

GREAT VEHICLE   *See* Vehicle.

GUANYIN (old spelling: Kuan Yin)   "The bodhisattva who hears the sounds of the world," who hears the groans and the cries for help, the embodiment of compassion, with a thousand hands and a thousand eyes, to whom people can turn in their troubles; depicted in East Asian iconography as a woman.

HUINENG (d. 714)   The sixth patriarch of Zen in China; also referred to by the name of his abode, Caoqi; also known as Workman Lu. Traditionally, he is said to have been an illiterate woodcutter who was enlightened when he happened to hear the *Diamond Sutra* being recited in the marketplace; he secretly received transmission from the fifth patriarch, after working as a lowly workman at his Zen monastery; in order to avoid the jealousy of other would-be claimants of his legacy, the fifth patriarch sent Huineng away in the middle of the night; Huineng returned to the south and dwelled in the mountains with hunters for many years before appearing in the world as a teacher.

THE IMPERATIVE The true imperative according to which Buddhist teaching must be carried out; teaching truth by means of truth without compromising with sentiments.

INDRA The king of the devas.

INTIMACY Openness to truth.

IRON OX Symbol of reality as a whole.

JADE RABBIT Symbol of the moon, of *yin;* *see* Yin-yang.

KARMA Deeds, action; Buddhism teaches that what is experienced is the result of past actions; karmic rewards for good deeds, karmic retribution for bad deeds.

KASHYAPA In the first transmission of Zen, Shakyamuni Buddha held up a flower to an assembly on Spirit Peak; Kashyapa gave a slight smile, indicating he understood Buddha's intent, so Buddha entrusted the eye of the correct teaching to him. Kashyapa is reckoned therefore as the first patriarch of Zen in India.

KINGLY WAY *See* Former Kings.

LI "Inner truth," "inner pattern" of things and events.

LINJI (d. 867) Seminal Zen master; his recorded sayings are a model of the precocious modernism of Zen talk; known for his shouts at students to break the continuity of their flow of delusion.

LION'S ROAR Symbol of the seeker's reaction to enlightenment, a roar of fearlessness and triumph.

MAITREYA   *See* Buddha.

MANJUSRI   Bodhisattva representing transcendent wisdom.

MIND   Frequent term in Zen, used in two senses: (1) the mind-ground, the One Mind, the ground of being, the buddha-mind, the mind of thusness: the all-pervasive ontological basis of all phenomena and beings; (2) false mind, the ordinary mind dominated by conditioning, desire, aversion, ignorance, and false sense of self, the mind of delusion; hence states of mind, attitudes, the mental moments of experience.

MOON   Solitary and round, a symbol of the One Mind. Without leaving the sky, the moon is reflected in the myriad streams, just as without changing or moving, the one reality pervades all particular experiences and events.

NAGAS   Serpents, dragons of the earth, seen as guardians of esoteric knowledge.

NIRMANAKAYA   *See* Buddha bodies.

NIRVANA   Peaceful extinction, the end of the cycle of birth and death, release from suffering. For bodhisattvas, nirvana is not experienced apart from the world of birth and death; in Great Vehicle Buddhism, clinging to nirvana is seen as the mark of the lesser vehicles.

PATCHROBED MONKS   Zen monks, who like the Sufis, had as their symbol the patched robe.

PATRIARCH   Term of respect used in the Zen school for the classic ancestral teachers of their tradition.

PEACH BLOSSOM SPRING   A magical utopia reached by lucky wanderers, a pristine land of uncrowded beauty and human simplicity. Described in a famous poem by Tao Yuanming.

PRAJNA   Transcendent wisdom, nonconceptual direct awareness; in Zen they say prajna is like a great mass of fire: whatever side you approach from, you get your face burned off; it is also like a pool of clear water, that can be entered from any side; as a moth can alight anywhere except in the flames of a fire, conditioned mind can become attached to anything, except to prajna.

PRIMORDIAL BUDDHA   The "first buddha" in the far, far past at the beginning of the present cosmic eon; used to symbolize the buddha-mind beyond space and time, reality prior to anything within our experience.

THE SAGE KINGS   *See* Former Kings.

SAMADHI   Stable meditative concentration; the states reached by Buddhist practitioners are sometimes termed samadhis; the adepts traverse countless samadhis.

SAMANTABHADRA   "The Universally Good One," the bodhisattva representing the good work of all the bodhisattvas in all worlds for the salvation of beings.

SAMBHOGAKAYA   *See* buddha bodies.

SAMSARA   *See* Birth and death.

SHAKYAMUNI   *See* Buddha.

SHAOLIN   *See* Bodhidharma.

SIDDHARTHA   *See* Buddha.

SON OF HEAVEN   The emperor of China, in his role as mediator between Heaven and the human world.

SPIRIT PEAK   Site of the first transmission of Zen; see Kashyapa.

STAFF   Symbol of the Zen teacher's authority to teach and power to make direct impact on students.

SUCHNESS   *See* Thusness.

SUMERU   In Indian cosmology, the polar mountain at the center of the world, surrounded by four continents and four oceans. In Zen, Sumeru often stands for the phenomenal world as a whole.

TAIPING   *See* Great Peace.

TATHAGATA   An epithet for a Buddha: one who has arrived at Thusness, and who has come from Thusness. *See* Thusness. With a capital *T*, Tathagata is an epithet of Shakyamuni Buddha.

TEN STAGES: The ten stages of a bodhisattva; described

in a book of *The Flower Ornament Scripture (Huayan Sutra)* (See the entry Bodhisattva for a bibliographic reference).

THAT SIDE   The absolute, immanent transcendent reality, Dharmakaya Buddha, buddha-mind, true thusness, "the other shore" reached by the enlightened.

THIS SIDE   The relative world, the world of interdependent causation, with temporary phenomena conditioning each other as cause and effect; the abode of impermanence, identitylessness, and suffering.

THUSNESS   Reality as it is, a fusion of noumenon and phenomenon, of absolute and relative. Another translation of the original term *tathata* is "suchness."

VAIROCANA   *See* Buddha.

VEHICLE   The Buddhist teachings are likened to vehicles for conveying sentient beings from delusion to enlightenment. Zen methods as a whole might be called the "vehicle of the Zen school" or perhaps the "supreme vehicle." In the Zen view, the lesser vehicles are those that seek personal salvation in escape from the world of suffering. The ideal of the Great Vehicle (Mahayana), and of the Zen school, is the bodhisattva, the enlightening being, who works for universal salvation.

VIMALAKIRTI   An enlightened layman, whose name means "Pure Name," the central figure of a sutra popular in East Asia; the prototype of a bodhisattva who combines transcendent wisdom with a life in the ordinary world.

WHITE SUN, BLUE SKY   Upon enlightenment, buddha-mind is as obvious and all-illuminating as the sun in a clear sky.

WIND   The pure wind is a symbol of the all-pervasive, ceaseless presence of the enlightening influence of reality; hence a symbol for the tradition of teachings that promotes enlightened awareness.

WORLD HONORED ONE   Epithet of Shakyamuni Buddha.

YAO and SHUN   *See* Former Kings.

YIN-YANG This pair of terms has many associations in traditional Chinese thought, for example:

yin: Dark, flexible, gentle, receptive

yang: Light, firm, strong, active

Zen people sometimes borrowed the terminology of Taoist spiritual alchemy, with meanings like this:

false *yin:* Body, desire, ignorance, human mind

true *yang:* Mind, reason, enlightenment, mind of Dao
Each term can have a dual sense: false *yin:* mundane, conditioned mind; true *yin:* quiescence, emptiness, receptivity; true *yang:* the inherent buddha-mind, primordial real consciousness; false *yang:* the impetuous misdirection of energy. See Thomas Cleary (trans.), *The Taoist I Ching* (Shambhala Publications, 1986).

YUNMEN (d. 949) Classic Zen teacher whose school continued for four centuries, preserving much Zen literature; noted for dazzling, arresting meditation sayings: "Take heaven and earth and put them on your eyelashes." "What is talk that goes beyond the buddhas and patriarchs? Cake." "What were the teachings of [Buddha's whole] lifetime? An appropriate statement."

ZHAOZHOU (778–897) Classic Zen master, one of whose famous sayings is, "Does a dog have buddha-nature? No."